SAVING DINNER THE VEGETARIAN WAY

SAVING
DINNER THE
VEGETARIAN
WAY

Healthy Menus, Recipes, and Shopping Lists to Keep Everyone Happy at the Table

LEANNE ELY

 BALLANTINE BOOKS · NEW YORK

A Ballantine Books Trade Paperback Original

Copyright © 2007 by Leanne Ely

Published in the United States by Ballantine Books, an imprint of The Random House
Publishing Group, a division of Random House, Inc., New York.

BALLANTINE and colophon are registered trademarks of Random House, Inc.

ISBN 978-0-345-48542-7

Library of Congress Cataloging-in-Publication Data
Ely, Leanne.
    Saving dinner the vegetarian way : healthy menus, recipes, and shopping lists to
keep everyone happy at the table / by Leanne Ely.
        p.   cm.
    ISBN 978-0-345-48542-7
    1. Vegetarian cookery.   2. Dinners and dining.   I. Title.
    TX837.E484 2007
    641.5'636—dc22   2006043081

Printed in the United States of America

www.ballantinebooks.com

9 8 7 6 5 4 3 2 1

Text design by Helene Berinsky

*This book is dedicated
to my parents, Miriam and Peter,
who kept our dinner table a sacred place.*

ACKNOWLEDGMENTS

Here it is again, folks. The famous (infamous?) Acknowledgments Page. This is where I get to do my acceptance speech and thank everyone and their mothers for everything ("I'd like to thank the Academy . . ."). Chances are good I will miss someone (I always do), but it just wouldn't feel like a *Saving Dinner* book if I didn't at least attempt it. So bear with me, here we go—

My husband, Dan, tells me he's just a common, simple man. If he is, he's *my* common, simple man and I adore him. His love and encouragement warm me daily, and I'm thankful for his stalwart presence and dependable nature.

My children Peter and Caroline have endured many books being written by their cookbook-writing mother and were just as patient with this one as they were with the other *Saving Dinner* books (NOT!). My new daughter, Meredith, has waded through this territory only once before and has found herself in the same camp as my other children, asking the same question, "Are you done yet?"

I don't know what else I can say about Marla Cilley (the FlyLady) that hasn't already been said. From my point of view, there simply couldn't be a better friend and mentor. We've been through a lot together, both personally and professionally. Marla is one of my most favorite people in the entire universe; I'm thankful to count her as one of my best friends.

Michelle Tessler, my wonderful agent, asked me to get off my duff and get another *Saving Dinner* book written, so I thank her for that inspiration along with the tons of Menu-Mailerettes who have requested a vegetarian version of *Saving Dinner* over the years. My editor, Caroline Sutton, has been through four of the five *Saving Dinner* books and could probably write the sixth one herself! Thanks, Caroline, for the terrific support and suggestions, as always.

A big thank you to the *Saving Dinner* staff, without whom I'd be totally lost! Kandi, my ever-capable, ever-patient, and amazing assistant; Tom, quiet, proficient, almost stealth helper with all things necessary; Bonnie, the brains and creativity behind our website, www.savingdinner.com; and the rest of our support team, Robyn, Nikki, Kimber, and Laura—a major thank you to each one of you for your loyalty, support, and hard work.

Lastly, I've dedicated this book to my parents because my mother taught me how to cook and my late father taught me to love it. It is my hope and prayer, regardless of your cooking persuasion (vegetarian or nonvegetarian) that you, too, will find joy in cooking and a love to create in your own kitchen.

CONTENTS

INTRODUCTION

A long time ago (about twenty-five years), in a world far, far away (one could say that about the 1980s), lived a young woman (that would be me) who decided (because of a man) to go vegetarian. Although there were countless vegetarian cookbooks available, the young woman instead opted for convenience and ate countless peanut butter sandwiches (natural peanut butter on whole-grain bread, mind you) and drank many a Dos Equis beer (no comment) with her paramour into the wee hours of the night. It was when she put on a hefty fifteen pounds that she decided being a vegetarian wasn't for her.

Fast forward to the twenty-first century. While I haven't become a full-fledged vegetarian twenty-plus years later, I do understand that the weight gain I experienced back then had to do with the robust nightly peanut butter sandwiches (yes, plural) and beers (also plural). And though my eating persuasion has stayed a more omnivorous course up to this point, I do recognize the value of eating vegetarian.

Vegetarianism used to be a 1970s tofu-Birkenstock-hippie experience that one eventually outgrew, as maturity and a more conventional life came into being. At least, that was the old way of looking at things.

But things have changed enormously in the last thirty-plus years. With as many as twenty-five million Americans calling themselves vegetarians, vegetarianism has gone mainstream, big time. The number of people becoming and staying vegetarian continues to grow, for a variety of reasons. From health concerns over Mad Cow disease, to ethical concerns about the way stock animals are raised, to the antibiotics, growth hormones, and the other stuff that goes into producing meat—all have contributed to a changed mind-set about "going veggie." No longer is vegetarianism associated with a quirky group of fringe folk. Today's vegetarians are the more ordinary people you meet every day, from all walks of life, choosing to live meatless: the family down the street, your doctor, the gal checking your groceries at the supermarket, and your babysitter, perhaps.

Regardless of one's affiliation with or without meat, the interest in vegetarian cooking, even part-time vegetarianism, and the demand from my readers are what propelled this book into being. *Saving Dinner the Vegetarian Way* is for all who are curious about how to cook veggie, who are trying to figure out ways to bring a family member's newfound vegetarianism to the dinner table, and who want a less meat-centered way of eating.

Vegetarianism, no matter how you define it—lacto (milk products allowed), ovo (eggs a-ok), lacto-ovo (yes to both), vegan (ix-nay on all animal products and for some this also means honey from bees)—offers an amazing array of delicious foods from every cultural and ethnic persuasion. And, as great fortune would have it, many of these fine dishes are quick and easy to prepare and do not require a trip to an obscure ethnic market or a day off from life to cook supper. This is easy, doable food for your busy family, done in the *Saving Dinner* tradition of offering you a balanced six-day weekly menu with different recipes, the itemized shopping list, and suggested side dishes.

Seeing families get back to the family dinner table has long been a passion of mine, and for many families, "going vegetarian" is a viable option, either part- or full-time. *Saving Dinner the Vegetarian Way* will certainly give you the tools to do it, plus keep your dinnertime engaging and its participants happy when the meal comes around, and that's what this book is truly all about.

The Care and Feeding of a Vegetarian

It's interesting, from my perspective as a nutritionist, how many people assume that just because they're vegetarians they are automatically eating "more nutritiously." This is far from true. The daughter of a dear friend of mine freaks me out—she won't touch vegetables, eats macaroni and cheese by the boatload, and has a big list of things she won't eat that have nothing to do with anything carnivore. She's just picky and her nutrition is atrocious! Another friend's friend thinks that because he's a vegetarian, he can drink unlimited martinis! Well, okay . . . gin and vodka would categorically fit into the vegetarian part of the food chain. However, grain alcohol will never count as a nutrient, whether you're a vegetarian or not.

In order to be the healthiest you can be, you should try to put away as many veggies each day as possible (not knock back as many martinis as possible). Salads should be excuses to cram in every vegetable from broccoli to zucchini, and this exercise should be done daily. Vegetables should be consumed in mass quantities—this is how healthy people live regardless of their affiliation with meat.

But the big concern for vegetarians is getting adequate amounts of protein. Like a lot of things in life, there is a formula for this. Keep in mind that you need to get about 15 percent of your daily calories from protein. Mathematically, that means you multiply your weight by 0.37 grams of protein to find out what your needs are. If you weigh 130 pounds, that would be $130 \times .37 = 48$ grams of protein needed per day. See how easy that is?

Nutrition labels are wonderful for helping you calculate how much you're getting, plus a few tricks like combining grains and beans will help you get higher counts and more complete proteins.

HOW TO USE THIS BOOK

Saving Dinner the Vegetarian Way is designed to give you everything you need to do dinner, as do my other *Saving Dinner* books. The recipes, serving suggestions, and, most important, categorized shopping lists are all contained within these pages. For your convenience, the grocery lists are also on the website, www.savingdinner.com, in an easy printable format.

The ingredients needed for the Serving Suggestions recipes are asterisked (**) on the grocery lists because I don't want you to feel obligated to follow any of my suggestions. I will tell you, however, that they are there for two reasons: (1) they are simple and delicious; (2) they help balance the nutrient count for the meal. So if you want to use them, great! If they don't strike your fancy, ignore them.

I strongly suggest you read the recipes before you hit the grocery store each week with the list. It helps to understand what you will be cooking that week before you head out the door to invest your hard-earned money in food from the grocery store. Those five minutes of reading through the recipes may help you make a quick decision if your store is out of something or you would prefer a substitute. You can't do that if you don't know what you're shopping for!

And like my other books, this book is crammed full of sidebars—read them! There is a ton of information to help you take full advantage of these menus and to make the recipes your own. As I was writing these recipes, I would think of something else that would empower you in the kitchen, and so I made a sidebar of the idea. The more equipped and knowledgeable you are, the faster you're able to make the recipes and do the shopping, and that makes your efforts worthwhile.

When appropriate, I have added Do Ahead Tips to help make cooking dinner quicker the next day (e.g., soaking the beans, precooking rice, potatoes, etc.). However, there are all kinds of things you can do the day before, if you so desire. I kept it basic; you might want to do more—it's totally up to you. You also can move days around if you want; just remember that the "Do Ahead" tips may no longer be appropriate if you do.

If you do want to make substitutions (accounting for allergies, preferences, etc.) on some of the grocery items, feel free! Maybe you and broccoli don't get along, but you love cauliflower; change it! Chances are good that the recipe will still work (maybe better—you just never know!). So, even though all the work of planning a menu has already been done for you, the Serving Suggestions are based on the season, and the grocery list is categorized, it doesn't mean that you can't make any changes. *Saving Dinner the Vegetarian Way* was written to empower your family at the dinner table every night—enjoy!

WINTER

❄ Week One

DAY ONE: Spicy Black Bean and Tofu Stew

DAY TWO: Broccoli Mushroom Noodle Casserole

DAY THREE: Bountiful Burritos

DAY FOUR: B-Cubed Salad (Beets, Blue Cheese, and
   Baby Greens)

DAY FIVE: Curried Stir-Fry

DAY SIX: Shepherd's Pie with Lentils

SHOPPING LIST

CONDIMENTS

Olive oil

Vegetable oil

Balsamic vinegar

Salsa, your favorite (2 cups)

Soy sauce, low-sodium if available

**Salad dressing, your choice (3 meals)

**Honey (1 meal)

**Mayonnaise (1 meal)

**Rice wine vinegar (1 meal)

PRODUCE

4 (14–16-ounce) packages firm tofu

5 pounds yellow onions

1 large red onion

2 garlic heads

1 bunch celery

3 medium green bell peppers

3 (8-ounce) packages mushrooms

1 bunch broccoli; **additional (1 meal)

2 heads cauliflower

8 ounces mixed baby greens

5–6 large russet potatoes

3 cups kale

2 large carrots

**Spinach (1 meal)

**Lettuce, not iceberg (2 meals)

**Baby carrots (1 meal)

**Salad toppings (see Salad Fixin's, page 252, for ideas;
   3 meals)

**Coleslaw mix (1 meal)

**Acorn squash (1 meal)

**Apples (1 meal)

CANNED GOODS

3 (14.5-ounce) cans low-sodium vegetable broth,
   if available

2 (14.5-ounce) cans Italian stewed tomatoes

1 (28-ounce) can whole tomatoes

3 (15-ounce) cans black beans

2 (14.5-ounce) cans vegetarian refried beans

2 (4.5-ounce) cans green chilies

2 (15-ounce) cans pickled beets

SPICES AND DRIED HERBS

Italian seasoning

Curry powder

Cinnamon

DAIRY/DAIRY CASE

Butter

Eggs (2)

Low-fat cottage cheese (3 cups)

Light sour cream (1 cup)

Shredded low-fat Cheddar cheese (1½ cups);
    **additional as slices (1 meal)

Shredded Monterey Jack cheese (1½ cups)

Crumbled blue cheese (4½ ounces)

DRY GOODS

Wide egg noodles (12 ounces)

Brown rice (1½ cups); **additional (1 meal)

Lentils, brown or green (1½ cups)

Bread crumbs (1½ cups)

BREAD/BAKERY

6 large whole wheat tortillas, 10 inches in diameter or
    burrito size

**Cornbread (1 meal)

**Whole wheat bread (1 meal)

SPICY BLACK BEAN AND TOFU STEW

Serves 6

1 large onion, chopped

2 teaspoons olive oil

2 (14–16-ounce) blocks firm tofu, drained and cubed

3 (15-ounce) cans black beans, with juice

2 (14.5-ounce) cans stewed tomatoes, Italian style, with juice

1 cup mild salsa

2 (4.5-ounce) cans chopped green chilies, drained

In a large skillet or Dutch oven, sauté onion in oil over medium heat.

Add cubed tofu and remaining ingredients. Cook over medium-low heat for 30 minutes.

PER SERVING:
387 Calories; 10g Fat; 26g Protein; 48g Carbohydrate; 16g Dietary Fiber; 0mg Cholesterol; 1120mg Sodium. Exchanges: 2 Grain (Starch); 4 Lean Meat; 3 Vegetable; 1 Fat.

SERVING SUGGESTIONS: Serve with a big spinach salad (see Salad Fixin's, page 252, for ideas) and cornbread with honey butter.

BROCCOLI MUSHROOM
NOODLE CASSEROLE

Serves 6

1 (12-ounce) package wide egg noodles
2 tablespoons butter
2 cups chopped onions
3 garlic cloves, pressed
1 large bunch broccoli, chopped
1 pound mushrooms, cleaned and sliced
Salt and pepper to taste
2 eggs, beaten
3 cups low-fat cottage cheese
1 cup light sour cream
1½ cups bread crumbs
1 cup shredded low-fat Cheddar cheese

Preheat oven to 350 degrees F. Grease a 9 × 13-inch baking pan.

Cook noodles for half the cooking time according to package directions. Drain and rinse under cold water. Drain again and set aside.

In a large skillet, melt butter over medium heat. Add onions and garlic and sauté for about 5 minutes. Add broccoli, mushrooms, salt, and pepper and continue cooking and stirring until broccoli is barely tender, about 3 minutes. Remove from heat.

In a large bowl, beat together eggs, cottage cheese, and sour cream. Add half-cooked noodles, sautéed vegetables, and 1 cup of bread crumbs. Mix well.

Pour into prepared pan and top with remaining bread crumbs. Cover and bake for 30 minutes. Uncover, sprinkle with shredded cheese, and bake for 15 more minutes.

PER SERVING:
578 Calories; 13g Fat; 38g Protein; 79g Carbohydrate; 7g Dietary Fiber; 147mg Cholesterol; 923mg Sodium. Exchanges: 4 Grain (Starch); 3 Lean Meat; 2½ Vegetable; 1 Fat; 0 Other Carbohydrates.

SERVING SUGGESTIONS: Serve with steamed baby carrots and a big green salad.

BOUNTIFUL BURRITOS

Serves 6

1 small onion, chopped
3 garlic cloves, pressed
1 cup chopped cauliflower
6 mushrooms, cleaned and chopped
1 medium green bell pepper, seeded, deribbed, and chopped
3 tablespoons olive oil
6 large whole wheat tortillas
2 (14.5-ounce) cans vegetarian refried beans
1½ cups shredded Monterey Jack cheese
1 cup jarred salsa (plus some for serving)
3 cups cooked brown rice

Preheat oven to 350 degrees F.

In a medium skillet, sauté onion, garlic, cauliflower, mushrooms, and pepper in oil over medium-high heat until onion is translucent. Set aside.

Lay tortillas down and spread a thin layer of refried beans, cheese, salsa, rice, and veggie mixture on each one. Roll up and put on cookie sheet.

Bake for 15 to 20 minutes. Serve topped with more salsa.

PER SERVING:
663 Calories; 22g Fat; 24g Protein; 91g Carbohydrate; 11g Dietary Fiber; 25mg Cholesterol; 1144mg Sodium. Exchanges: 5½ Grain (Starch); 1½ Lean Meat; 1 Vegetable; 3½ Fat.

SERVING SUGGESTION: Serve with coleslaw (use ready-made coleslaw mix and add mayonnaise and a dash of rice vinegar).

B-CUBED SALAD (BEETS, BLUE CHEESE, AND BABY GREENS)

Serves 6

"This one is a TOTAL 10! This recipe was fabulous, easy, and definitely a great break from the stove. Tasted wonderful (always a fan of blue cheese). Thanks!"   —Debi from Texas

> 8 ounces mixed baby greens
> 1½ (15-ounce) cans pickled beets, drained (save remaining beets to
>   add in a side salad this week)
> 4½ ounces crumbled blue cheese
> 1 red onion, cut into thin slices and halved
> 4½ tablespoons olive oil
> 1½ tablespoons balsamic vinegar
> Salt and pepper to taste

In a large bowl, combine baby greens, beets, blue cheese, and onion.

In a small bowl or cup, mix olive oil and balsamic vinegar. Add salt and pepper.

Pour dressing over salad and toss.

PER SERVING:
222 Calories; 16g Fat; 6g Protein; 14g Carbohydrate; 3g Dietary Fiber; 16mg Cholesterol; 457mg Sodium. Exchanges: ½ Grain (Starch); ½ Lean Meat; 1 Vegetable; 0 Fruit; 3 Fat.

SERVING SUGGESTIONS: Serve with grilled Cheddar and apple sandwiches on whole wheat bread.

CURRIED STIR-FRY

Serves 6

2 medium onions, chopped
2 garlic cloves, pressed
1½ pounds tofu, drained and cubed
2 tablespoons vegetable oil
3 cups stemmed and chopped kale
2 tablespoons curry powder (or to taste)
⅓ teaspoon ground cinnamon
2¼ cups vegetable broth
1 large head cauliflower, trimmed into florets and chopped
2 medium green bell peppers, seeded, deribbed, and chopped
Low-sodium soy sauce to taste

In a large skillet or wok, stir-fry onions, garlic, and tofu in oil. Continue to stir-fry until tofu is lightly browned, about 4 minutes. Remove from skillet and keep warm.

Add kale to pan. Stir-fry till bright green, then add curry powder and cinnamon. Stir again before adding ⅓ vegetable broth. Cover and let simmer on medium heat for about 2 minutes.

Uncover skillet or wok and add cauliflower, bell peppers, and soy sauce to taste.

Stir and add ¾ cup vegetable broth and continue cooking until kale and cauliflower are tender, about 3 minutes. Add remaining vegetable broth as needed to keep stir-fry from sticking.

PER SERVING:
227 Calories; 11g Fat; 14g Protein; 23g Carbohydrate; 6g Dietary Fiber; 1mg Cholesterol; 642mg Sodium. Exchanges: ½ Grain (Starch); 1 Lean Meat; 1½ Vegetable; 1½ Fat; 0 Other Carbohydrates.

SERVING SUGGESTIONS: Serve on a bed of brown rice and add a big green salad.

DO AHEAD TIP: Make 4 cups of mashed potatoes for tomorrow night's meal.

SHEPHERD'S PIE WITH LENTILS

Serves 6

1 tablespoon vegetable oil
2 medium onions, finely chopped
4 celery stalks, thinly sliced
2 large carrots, peeled and thinly sliced
2 garlic cloves, pressed
Salt and pepper to taste
½ teaspoon Italian seasoning
1½ cups brown or green lentils, rinsed
1 (28-ounce) can tomatoes, coarsely chopped
2 cups vegetable broth

TOPPING

4 cups mashed potatoes
½ cup shredded low-fat Cheddar cheese

In a large skillet, heat oil over medium heat. Add onions, celery, and carrots and sauté for about 7 minutes, until veggies are soft. Add garlic, salt, pepper, and Italian seasoning and continue cooking for about 1 minute.

Add lentils and tomatoes with juice and bring to a boil. Transfer to slow cooker and stir in vegetable broth.

Spread mashed potatoes* evenly over lentil mixture. Sprinkle with Cheddar cheese. Cover and cook on low for 6 to 7 hours or on high for 3 to 4 hours.

*Cook's Note: If you are using mashed potatoes with milk in them, do not add the potatoes until the last 30 minutes. Cook on high for 30 minutes, until potatoes are hot and the cheese has melted.

PER SERVING:
426 Calories; 10g Fat; 22g Protein; 64g Carbohydrate; 21g Dietary Fiber; 14mg Cholesterol; 968mg Sodium. Exchanges: 3½ Grain (Starch); 1½ Lean Meat; 1½ Vegetable; 2 Fat.

SERVING SUGGESTIONS: Serve with steamed broccoli and baked acorn squash.

❄ Week Two

DAY ONE: Italian Pasta and Bean Bake
DAY TWO: Cheesy Faux Soufflé
DAY THREE: Gingered Stir-Fry
DAY FOUR: Lentil Soup
DAY FIVE: Asian Salad
DAY SIX: Tempeh Stuffed Peppers

SHOPPING LIST

CONDIMENTS

Olive oil

Vegetable oil

Red wine vinegar

Balsamic vinegar

Vinegar (if not using white wine)

White wine (if not using white grape juice)

White grape juice (if not using white wine)

Soy sauce, low-sodium if available

**Salad dressing, your choice (4 meals)

PRODUCE

6 ounces tempeh

3 pounds yellow onions (keep on hand)

2 bunches green onions

2 heads garlic

6 large green bell peppers

1 bunch celery

1 pound carrots

3 cups snow peas

1 pound green beans

1 head cauliflower

1 head broccoli

1 (8–10-ounce) bag shredded red cabbage

2-inch piece ginger root

1 bunch parsley

3–5 large limes (for ½ cup juice)

**Lettuce, not iceberg (2 meals)

**Spinach (2 meals)

**Salad toppings, your choice (4 meals)

**Sweet potatoes (1 meal)

**Kale (1 meal)

CANNED GOODS

4 (14.5-ounce) cans low-sodium vegetable broth

5 (14.5-ounce) cans diced tomatoes

2 (16-ounce) cans kidney beans

1 (26-ounce) can/jar pasta sauce, your favorite

SPICES AND DRIED HERBS

Italian seasoning

Thyme

Basil

Garlic powder

**Cinnamon

DAIRY/DAIRY CASE

Butter

Eggs (4)

Shredded Cheddar cheese (2½ cups)

Mozzarella cheese (8 ounces)

Ricotta cheese (2 cups)

**Sour cream, garnish (1 meal)

DRY GOODS

Flour

Arrowroot or cornstarch

Brown sugar

Sugar

Penne pasta (1 pound)

Brown rice (2¼ cups); **additional (1 meal)

Lentils (1½ cups)

Bread crumbs (¾ cup)

Pine nuts (½ cup)

Ramen noodles (3 packages)

BREADS/BAKERY

**Corn muffins (1 meal)

**Whole-grain rolls (2 meals)

1 loaf French bread

ITALIAN PASTA AND BEAN BAKE

Serves 6

1 pound penne pasta
1 (14.5-ounce) can diced tomatoes, drained
2 (16-ounce) cans kidney beans, rinsed and drained
1 (26-ounce) jar pasta sauce
1 teaspoon Italian seasoning
8 ounces shredded mozzarella cheese

Preheat oven to 375 degrees F.

Prepare pasta according to package directions until al dente. Drain and return to pot. Add tomatoes, beans, pasta sauce, Italian seasoning, and ½ of the cheese.

Transfer to an 11 × 7-inch baking dish.

Bake for 25 minutes. Sprinkle remaining cheese on top and bake an additional 15 minutes or until the cheese melts.

PER SERVING:
580 Calories; 11g Fat; 28g Protein; 93g Carbohydrate; 10g Dietary Fiber; 34mg Cholesterol; 1125mg Sodium. Exchanges: 5 Grain (Starch); 1½ Lean Meat; 2½ Vegetable; 1 Fat.

SERVING SUGGESTIONS: Serve with a large green salad and some garlic bread.

CHEESY FAUX SOUFFLÉ

2 cups ricotta cheese
¾ cup bread crumbs
½ cup flour
⅓ cup chopped fresh parsley
⅓ cup chopped green onions
2 tablespoons butter, softened
Salt and pepper to taste
4 eggs

Preheat oven to 350 degrees F. Lightly grease a 5-cup soufflé or casserole dish.

In a mixing bowl, blend together ricotta cheese, bread crumbs, flour, parsley, green onions, butter, salt, and pepper. Set aside.

In separate mixing bowl, beat eggs with an electric mixer or by hand until thickened. Fold ricotta cheese mixture into eggs.

Pour egg mixture into soufflé or casserole dish. Bake for about 1 hour or until knife inserted comes out clean.

PER SERVING:
320 Calories; 19g Fat; 16g Protein; 21g Carbohydrate; 1g Dietary Fiber; 193mg Cholesterol; 274mg Sodium. Exchanges: 1 Grain (Starch); 2 Lean Meat; 0 Vegetable; 2½ Fat.

SERVING SUGGESTIONS: Serve with a spinach salad and corn muffins.

GINGERED STIR-FRY

Serves 6

1½ cups water

⅓ cup white wine (or white grape juice with a splash of vinegar)

3 tablespoons low-sodium soy sauce

2 tablespoons arrowroot or cornstarch

¾ teaspoon brown sugar

1½ tablespoons vegetable oil

1 tablespoon grated ginger root

1 pound green beans, stringed and cut diagonally

2 cups cauliflower florets

2 cups broccoli florets

4 green onions, chopped

½ cup pine nuts

Mix water, wine, soy sauce, arrowroot, and brown sugar. Stir well to dissolve brown sugar. Set aside.

In a wok or large skillet, heat oil over medium-high heat. Add ginger and stir-fry for about 20 seconds or till fragrant. Add beans, cauliflower, broccoli, and green onions and cook for about 3 minutes, or until veggies are tender. Remove veggies from skillet.

Add sauce to skillet and allow it to thicken for about 2 minutes. Return veggies to wok or skillet and stir to coat in sauce. Cook 1 to 2 minutes or until all ingredients are heated through.

Garnish with pine nuts and serve.

PER SERVING:
169 Calories; 10g Fat; 8g Protein; 15g Carbohydrate; 5g Dietary Fiber; 0mg Cholesterol; 322mg Sodium. Exchanges: 0 Grain (Starch); ½ Lean Meat; 2 Vegetable; 1½ Fat; 0 Other Carbohydrates.

SERVING SUGGESTIONS: Serve on a bed of brown rice and add a nice, big green salad.

DO AHEAD TIP: Cook 1½ cups lentils for tomorrow night's meal.

LENTIL SOUP

"This soup scores an 8 even when we forgot the red wine vinegar! Good basic lentil veggie soup. But it scores a 10 with the red wine vinegar! Amazing difference!"
　　　　　　　　　　　　　　　　　　　　　　　　—Jennifer N.

　　　2 tablespoons olive oil
　　　6 garlic cloves, pressed
　　　2 cups chopped onions
　　　2 celery stalks, chopped
　　　3 carrots, sliced
　　　6 cups low-sodium vegetable broth
　　　2 (14.5-ounce) cans diced tomatoes
　　　1½ cups lentils, rinsed
　　　1 teaspoon dried thyme
　　　Salt and pepper to taste
　　　2 tablespoons red wine vinegar

In a large soup pot, heat olive oil over medium-high heat. Add garlic and onions and sauté for 4 minutes or until onions are translucent. Add celery, carrots, broth, tomatoes, lentils, thyme, and salt and pepper and bring to a boil. Reduce heat to low and simmer for 30 minutes or until carrots are soft.

Ladle hot soup into bowls, topping off with a drizzle of red wine vinegar.

PER SERVING:
215 Calories; 1g Fat; 22g Protein; 33g Carbohydrate; 14g Dietary Fiber; 0mg Cholesterol; 549mg Sodium. Exchanges: 1½ Grain (Starch); 2 Lean Meat; 2 Vegetable; 0 Fat; 0 Other Carbohydrates.

SERVING SUGGESTIONS: Serve with whole-grain rolls and a spinach salad.

ASIAN SALAD

Serves 6

4½ quarts water
Salt to taste
3 cups snow peas
3 packages ramen noodles (discard flavor packets)
1 (8–10-ounce) bag shredded red cabbage (about 3 cups)
3 cups shredded carrots
1½ cups sliced celery
¾ cup chopped green onions

DRESSING

⅔ cup olive oil
½ cup fresh lime juice
2 teaspoons sugar
3 tablespoons grated ginger root
¾ teaspoon garlic powder
3 teaspoons low-sodium soy sauce
3 tablespoons balsamic vinegar
Salt and pepper to taste

In a large saucepan, bring water and salt to a boil. Meanwhile, trim and string snow peas. When water is at a rolling boil, add ramen noodles, stirring to separate noodles, and then add snow peas. Cook for 3 minutes. Drain and rinse under cold water immediately.

In a large salad bowl, combine red cabbage, carrots, celery, and green onions; toss to mix. Add noodles and snow peas, and toss until well mixed.

In a large measuring cup, mix dressing ingredients and stir with a fork (or just throw all that stuff in a jar with a lid and shake). Pour dressing over the salad and toss to coat.

PER SERVING:
281 Calories; 24g Fat; 3g Protein; 16g Carbohydrate; 4g Dietary Fiber; 0mg Cholesterol; 174mg Sodium. Exchanges: 0 Grain (Starch); 2½ Vegetable; 0 Fruit; 5 Fat; 0 Other Carbohydrates.

SERVING SUGGESTIONS: Serve with whole-grain rolls and baked sweet potatoes.

TEMPEH STUFFED PEPPERS

6 ounces tempeh, cubed
2 garlic cloves, pressed
2 (14.5-ounce) cans diced tomatoes
2 teaspoons dried basil
1 small onion, chopped
4½ cups cooked brown rice
2½ cups shredded Cheddar cheese
6 large green bell peppers, tops removed and seeded

In a saucepan, steam the tempeh for 10 minutes. In a bowl, mash steamed tempeh, garlic, 1 can of the tomatoes, and basil.

Stir in onion, rice, and 2 cups of cheese. Stuff the tempeh-rice mixture into peppers.

Place stuffed peppers in the bottom of a slow cooker (as many as you can on bottom and the rest on top of those). Pour remaining can of tomatoes over peppers.

Cover and cook on low for 6 to 8 hours or on high for 3 to 4 hours. Sprinkle peppers with remaining cheese the last 30 minutes of cooking.

PER SERVING:
575 Calories; 22g Fat; 25g Protein; 72g Carbohydrate; 4g Dietary Fiber; 55mg Cholesterol; 335mg Sodium. Exchanges: 4 Grain (Starch); 2½ Lean Meat; 2 Vegetable; 2½ Fat.

SERVING SUGGESTIONS: Serve with sautéed kale and a dollop of sour cream on top of the peppers.

❄ Week Three

DAY ONE: Tri-Cheesy Stuffed Shells

DAY TWO: Soft Tofacos

DAY THREE: Caribbean Black Bean Soup

DAY FOUR: Cauliflower and Pasta Bake

DAY FIVE: Lentil Nut Loaf

DAY SIX: Hearty Beans

SHOPPING LIST

CONDIMENTS

Olive oil

Vegetable oil

Vegetarian Worcestershire sauce

Ketchup

Salsa (garnish)

**Salad dressing, your favorite (3 meals)

**Honey (1 meal)

**Mayonnaise (1 meal)

PRODUCE

2 (14–16-ounce) packages extra-firm tofu

3 pounds yellow onions (keep on hand)

3 large red onions

2 garlic heads; **additional (1 meal)

1 green bell pepper

Mushrooms (1 cup)

2 medium tomatoes

1 medium carrot; **1 bag carrots or 1 bag shredded carrots

1 large russet potato

1 head lettuce (you'll need 2 cups shredded)

1 bunch basil

1 bunch cilantro

1 lemon

**Lettuce, not iceberg (2 meals)

**Baby greens (1 meal)

**Salad toppings (3 meals)

**Baby carrots (1 meal)

**Kale (1 meal)

**Hubbard squash (1 meal)

**Acorn squash (1 meal)

**Swiss chard (1 meal)

CANNED GOODS

3 (14.5-ounce) cans low-sodium vegetable broth

1 (14.5-ounce) can diced tomatoes

1 (28-ounce) can whole tomatoes

2 (14-ounce) cans fat-free refried beans

2 (15-ounce) cans black beans

2 (14.5-ounce) cans white kidney beans

1 (4-ounce) can green chilies

1 (26-ounce) jar pasta sauce, your favorite

SPICES AND DRIED HERBS

Parsley

Marjoram

Rosemary

Cumin

Cayenne pepper

2 (1.25-ounce) packages taco seasoning mix

DAIRY/DAIRY CASE

Butter

Eggs (3)

Milk (4 cups)

1 (8-ounce) container light sour cream

1 (15-ounce) container low-fat cottage cheese

Shredded mozzarella cheese (2 cups)

Grated Parmesan cheese (2⅓ cups)

Shredded low-fat Cheddar cheese (2 cups)

DRY GOODS

Flour

Brown sugar

Jumbo pasta shells (18)

Penne pasta (1 pound)

Lentils (1¼ cups)

Bread crumbs (1 cup)

1 cup nuts (pecans, walnuts, or your favorite)

**Brown rice (1 meal)

**Raisins (1 meal)

**Chopped walnuts (1 meal)

BREADS/BAKERY

12 whole wheat tortillas

5 slices whole wheat bread

**Garlic bread (1 meal)

**Corn muffins (2 meals)

FROZEN FOODS

1 (10-ounce) package chopped broccoli

2 (16-ounce) packages cauliflower florets

Serves 6

18 jumbo pasta shells
1 (15-ounce) container low-fat cottage cheese
1 (10-ounce) package frozen chopped broccoli, thawed and drained
2 cups shredded mozzarella cheese
⅓ cup grated Parmesan cheese
1 egg, beaten
2 tablespoons dried parsley
Salt and pepper to taste
1 (26-ounce) jar pasta sauce

Preheat oven to 400 degrees F. Lightly grease a 9 × 13-inch casserole dish.

Cook pasta shells according to package directions until al dente; drain and keep warm.

Meanwhile, combine cottage cheese, broccoli, 1 cup mozzarella cheese, Parmesan cheese, beaten egg, parsley, and salt and pepper. Gently stir until all ingredients are well mixed.

Spoon 2 tablespoons of filling into each shell. In the bottom of baking dish, spread 1 cup of pasta sauce. Place shells on top of the sauce in one layer. Pour remaining sauce over the shells. Sprinkle with remaining mozzarella cheese. Bake for 25 minutes or until bubbling hot.

PER SERVING:
307 Calories; 13g Fat; 24g Protein; 23g Carbohydrate; 2g Dietary Fiber; 76mg Cholesterol; 554mg Sodium. Exchanges: 1 Grain (Starch); 3 Lean Meat; ½ Vegetable; 1½ Fat.

SERVING SUGGESTIONS: A nice, big green salad and garlic bread would be wonderful. Put a bowl of baby carrots on the table for an extra crunch.

SOFT TOFACOS

Serves 6

4 tablespoons vegetable oil
2 (14–16-ounce) packages extra-firm tofu, drained and crumbled
2 (1.25-ounce) packages taco seasoning mix
1 cup water
12 whole wheat tortillas
2 (14-ounce) cans fat-free refried beans
2 medium tomatoes, chopped
2 cups shredded lettuce
2 cups shredded low-fat Cheddar cheese
Light sour cream
Salsa

In a large saucepan, heat oil over medium heat. Add chunks of tofu, crumbling them with a fork. Cook for 10 minutes. Add taco seasoning packets and water. Stir, coating tofu, and cook until sauce is thickened.

Meanwhile, wrap tortillas in foil and heat in 350 degree F. oven for 10 minutes. Also, in a saucepan, heat refried beans.

To serve, spread each tortilla with a layer of refried beans. Add several heaping spoonfuls of tofu. Add chopped tomatoes, lettuce, and cheese. Top with a dollop of sour cream and salsa.

PER SERVING:
722 Calories; 25g Fat; 38g Protein; 87g Carbohydrate; 13g Dietary Fiber; 11mg Cholesterol; 2422mg Sodium. Exchanges: 1½ Grain (Starch); 5 Lean Meat; ½ Vegetable; 2½ Fat; ½ Other Carbohydrates.

SERVING SUGGESTION: Serve with a big green salad.

Serves 6

1 tablespoon olive oil
2 large onions, chopped
6 garlic cloves, pressed
1 medium carrot, diced
1 medium green bell pepper, seeded, deribbed, and chopped
1–2 teaspoons cumin, depending on your preference
2 (15-ounce) cans black beans, drained but not rinsed
1 (14.5-ounce) can vegetable broth
1 (14.5-ounce) can diced tomatoes
1 (4-ounce) can green chilies, chopped
Salt and pepper to taste
½ cup light sour cream

In a large soup pot, heat olive oil over medium heat. Add onions, garlic, carrot, and green bell pepper and cook, stirring often, for about 4 minutes.

Increase heat and add cumin, beans, broth, tomatoes, and green chilies. Season with salt and pepper. Bring to a boil. Cover, lower heat to medium, and simmer for about 10 minutes. Ladle into soup bowls and serve with a dollop of sour cream.

PER SERVING:
653 Calories; 7g Fat; 37g Protein; 115g Carbohydrate; 26g Dietary Fiber; 5mg Cholesterol; 592mg Sodium. Exchanges: 6½ Grain (Starch); 2 Lean Meat; 2 Vegetable; 1 Fat; 0 Other Carbohydrates.

SERVING SUGGESTION: Serve with a salad of baby greens and corn muffins.

CAULIFLOWER AND PASTA BAKE

Serves 6

> 1 pound penne pasta
> 1¼ (16-ounce) packages frozen cauliflower florets
> 2 tablespoons olive oil
> 2 red onions, chopped
> 2 garlic cloves, pressed
> 5 tablespoons butter
> 4 tablespoons flour
> 4 cups milk
> 2 cups freshly grated Parmesan cheese
> ½ cup firmly packed and shredded fresh basil
> ½ teaspoon cayenne pepper, or to taste
> 5 slices whole wheat bread, crusts removed
> 4 tablespoons butter, melted

Preheat oven to 350 degrees F. Lightly grease a 9 × 13-inch casserole dish.

Prepare pasta according to package directions until al dente; drain and set aside.

Steam cauliflower until just tender, according to package directions.

In a skillet, heat oil over medium-high heat; add onions and garlic and cook till soft, about 4 minutes. Transfer onions and garlic to a mixing bowl. Add steamed cauliflower to bowl and stir to combine.

In the same skillet, melt butter. Blend in flour and, stirring constantly, cook for 1 minute. Gradually whisk in milk. Stir constantly until mixture boils and thickens. Remove from heat and add 1¼ cups of Parmesan cheese, basil, and cayenne. Add cauliflower, onions, garlic, and pasta to the sauce; mix well.

Spoon cauliflower mixture into baking dish. Cut bread into large cubes. Coat cubes with melted butter and scatter them over the top of casserole. Sprinkle with remaining Parmesan cheese. Bake for 35 to 40 minutes, until the top is slightly browned.

PER SERVING:
622 Calories; 37g Fat; 25g Protein; 50g Carbohydrate; 5g Dietary Fiber; 90mg Cholesterol; 890mg Sodium. Exchanges: 2 Grain (Starch); 1½ Lean Meat; 2 Vegetable; ½ Non-Fat Milk; 6 Fat.

SERVING SUGGESTIONS: Serve with braised kale and baked Hubbard squash.

DO AHEAD TIP: Cook lentils for tomorrow night's meal.

Lentils: The Ultimate Fast-Food Legume

Delicious, earthy, and wonderfully fragrant—no wonder Esau lost his birthright over a big bowl of lentil soup!

Lentils aren't your typical bean or legume, requiring overnight soaking and hours of cooking. No, lentils are, hands-down, a quick and dirty way to get dinner happening without the fuss of a traditional bean dish. And they are healthy: 1 cup of cooked lentils is chock-full of protein, calcium, magnesium, potassium, iron, and a colossal amount of fiber—10 whole grams!

Making lentils couldn't be easier. Here's the lowdown on making lentil cuisine:

Like any dried bean, once you've opened the bag to get them ready to cook, you need to sort through them and make sure you don't have any rocks, bugs, or other non-lentil items present in your legumes.

Next, you need to rinse them to get any residual dirt off. This is best done in a colander or sieve (some colanders work well; others have holes that are too big and the lentils slip through, so a sieve is better). Rinse the lentils with cool water several times, stirring them so to speak, with your hand in the colander to get them nice and clean. Now place the cleaned lentils in a large saucepan or soup pot. To about 2 cups of cleaned lentils, add 6 cups of water or vegetable stock. Bring the pot to a boil. As the water boils, the lentils will begin to foam—the foam looks kind of like dirty bath suds! You will definitely want to remove the foam off the top of your boiling pot with a slotted spoon and discard. Lower the heat and let the lentils simmer, about 20 minutes. You want them to be firm and to hold their shape yet still be cooked and tender. Sound complicated? It's really not—you just need to test the lentils after about 20 minutes to make sure you're on track.

Once your lentils are cooked and recipe-ready, proceed to the next cooking step and enjoy this healthy legume!

LENTIL NUT LOAF

2 tablespoons olive oil
1 large onion, chopped
1 cup chopped mushrooms
2½ cups cooked lentils
1 cup nuts, ground (pecans, walnuts, or your favorite)
1 cup bread crumbs
1 tablespoon lemon juice
1 tablespoon vegetarian Worcestershire sauce
1 tablespoon dried marjoram
2 eggs, beaten
Salt and pepper to taste

TOPPING (OPTIONAL)

½ cup ketchup
2 tablespoons brown sugar

Preheat oven to 350 degrees F. Lightly grease an 8-inch loaf pan.

In a skillet, heat oil over medium-high heat and sauté onion and mushrooms until soft, about 4 minutes.

In a large bowl, combine sautéed veggies with remaining ingredients. Mix well and form into a loaf. Place in loaf pan and bake for 30 minutes.

Mix topping ingredients. About 15 minutes before loaf is ready to come out of oven, spread topping onto loaf and continue baking for remaining time.

PER SERVING:
391 Calories; 21g Fat; 16g Protein; 38g Carbohydrate; 10g Dietary Fiber; 71mg Cholesterol; 209mg Sodium. Exchanges: 2½ Grain (Starch); 1½ Lean Meat; ½ Vegetable; 0 Fruit; 3½ Fat; 0 Other Carbohydrates.

SERVING SUGGESTIONS: Serve with braised Swiss chard and baked acorn squash.

HEARTY BEANS

Serves 6

1 tablespoon olive oil
1 large red onion
4 garlic cloves, pressed
1 large russet potato, peeled and grated
1 tablespoon dried rosemary
Salt and pepper to taste
1 (28-ounce) can whole tomatoes, coarsely chopped
2 (14.5-ounce) cans white kidney beans, drained and rinsed
2 (14.5-ounce) cans low-sodium vegetable broth
¼ cup whole cilantro leaves

In a skillet, heat oil over medium heat. Add onion and cook until soft, about 4 minutes. Add garlic, potato, rosemary, and salt and pepper. Cook for 1 minute, stirring frequently. Stir in tomatoes and bring to a boil. Cook, stirring, for about 2 minutes.

Add beans to slow cooker. Pour tomato mixture over beans and mix well. Add vegetable broth, barely to cover. Cover and cook on low for 8 to 10 hours or on high for 4 to 5 hours. Stir in cilantro leaves and serve.

PER SERVING:
260 Calories; 3g Fat; 17g Protein; 44g Carbohydrate; 10g Dietary Fiber; 0mg Cholesterol; 418mg Sodium. Exchanges: 2 Grain (Starch); 1 Lean Meat; 1½ Vegetable; ½ Fat.

SERVING SUGGESTIONS: Serve on a bed of brown rice and with Carrot Slaw (see page 254), and corn muffins and honey butter on the side.

❄ Week Four

DAY ONE: Winter Vegetable Lasagna

DAY TWO: Easy Tofu and Vegetables

DAY THREE: Warm Bean Salad

DAY FOUR: Cream of Peanut Soup

DAY FIVE: Hoppin' John

DAY SIX: Sweet-and-Sour Cabbage

SHOPPING LIST

CONDIMENTS

Olive oil

Balsamic vinegar

Soy sauce, low-sodium, if available

Chili purée with garlic (often found in the Asian section)

Honey

Peanut butter, creamy (1¼ cups)

**Salad dressing, your choice (2 meals)

**Mayonnaise

**Toasted sesame oil

**Vinaigrette dressing (I like Paul Newman's Balsamic
   Vinaigrette)

**Rice vinegar

PRODUCE

2 (14–16-ounce) packages firm tofu

3 pounds yellow onions (keep on hand)

2 bunches green onions

1 garlic head

1 large red bell pepper

1 bunch celery

Mushrooms (18 whole mushrooms to slice + 3 ounces; or
   an 8-ounce container of presliced mushrooms)

2 medium carrots

1 bunch bok choy (for 6 cups chopped)

Butternut squash (1 pound)

5 ounces green beans

6 cups spinach; **additional (1 meal)

1 head green cabbage

1-inch piece ginger root

1 bunch parsley

1 bunch cilantro; **additional (1 meal)

4 tart apples

2–3 lemons (you'll need ¼ cup juice)

**Salad toppings (2 meals)

**Baby greens (1 meal)

**Collard greens (1 meal)

**Baby carrots (1 meal)

**Sweet potatoes (1 meal)

**1 bag coleslaw mix (1 meal)

**Salad veggies (clean out your crisper!; 1 meal)

CANNED GOODS

4 (14.5-ounce) cans low-sodium vegetable broth

1 (16-ounce) can diced tomatoes

2 (16-ounce) cans black-eyed peas

2 (16-ounce) cans mixed beans (combination of pinto,
   kidney, and great northern)

Apple juice (¼ cup)

SPICES AND DRIED HERBS

Basil

Thyme

Celery seed

Allspice

Butter

Low-fat milk (1 quart)

½ pint half-and-half

Shredded part-skim mozzarella cheese (2 cups)

Grated Parmesan cheese (¼ cup)

**Blue cheese crumbles (1 meal)

DRY GOODS

Flour

Cornstarch

Brown sugar

Lasagna noodles (1 pound)

Brown rice (1½ cups); **additional (2 meals)

Pine nuts (¼ cup)

Peanuts (14)

Golden raisins (½ cup)

**Barley (1 meal)

**Whole wheat couscous (1 meal)

**Dry-roasted peanuts (1 meal)

**Pasta (fusilli works great; 1 meal)

BREADS/BAKERY

**Whole-grain bread (1 meal)

WINTER VEGETABLE LASAGNA

Serves 6

1 pound lasagna noodles
2 tablespoons butter
1 large onion, diced
1 pound butternut squash, peeled and diced
2 medium carrots, peeled and diced
½ cup flour
3 cups low-fat milk
½ cup golden raisins
Salt and pepper to taste
2 cups shredded part-skim mozzarella cheese
¼ cup grated Parmesan cheese
¼ cup pine nuts

Preheat oven to 350 degrees F.

Cook lasagna noodles according to package directions until al dente; drain.

In large saucepan, melt butter over low heat. Add onion, squash, and carrots. Cook vegetables over low heat until very soft, about 5 minutes. If vegetable mixture starts to stick to the pan, you might have to add a little water to keep it from sticking—about ¼ cup is adequate.

Once veggies are tender, stir in flour. Gradually stir in milk, and keep stirring until mixture is smooth. Bring mixture to a boil and then stir in raisins, and salt and pepper. You will have a nice veggie sauce with minimal lumps and bumps. Remove from heat. Set aside 1 cup of this mixture for a later use.

In a 9 × 13-inch baking dish, spread a little of the vegetable sauce over the bottom and cover with noodles. Sprinkle mozzarella over noodles and add more vegetable sauce. Continue to layer sauce, mozzarella, and noodles, ending with a cup of reserved sauce. Sprinkle top with Parmesan and nuts. Bake, uncovered, for 40 minutes.

PER SERVING:
653 Calories; 18g Fat; 29g Protein; 95g Carbohydrate; 5g Dietary Fiber; 42mg Cholesterol; 380mg Sodium. Exchanges: 5 Grain (Starch); 2 Lean Meat; 1 Vegetable; ½ Fruit; ½ Non-Fat Milk; 2 Fat.

SERVING SUGGESTION: Serve with a nice, big spinach salad.

EASY TOFU AND VEGETABLES

Serves 6

> 3 tablespoons olive oil
> 1½ (14–16-ounce) packages firm tofu, drained and cubed
> 6 celery stalks, chopped
> 18 mushrooms, cleaned and sliced
> 2 garlic cloves, pressed
> 6 cups chopped bok choy
> 1 (14.5-ounce) can low-sodium vegetable broth
> ¼ cup low-sodium soy sauce
> ½–1 tablespoon chili purée with garlic (more or less depending on
>   heat tolerance)
> 2 tablespoons cornstarch
> 1 tablespoon brown sugar
> 1 tablespoon finely grated ginger root
> 9 stalks green onions, chopped
> 6 cups coarsely chopped fresh spinach
> Salt and pepper to taste

In a Dutch oven or large skillet, heat oil over medium-high heat. Add tofu and sauté for a few minutes till almost golden brown, about 3 minutes. Then add celery, mushrooms, and garlic and sauté until tofu is browned, about 3 to 4 minutes. Add bok choy, cover with a lid, and cook an additional 10 minutes or until bok choy is nearly tender.

In a small bowl, whisk together the broth, soy sauce, chili purée, cornstarch, brown sugar, and ginger. Pour over the vegetables and stir together, allowing mixture to come to a simmer.

Add green onions and spinach. Season with salt (if needed) and pepper. Cover and cook for about 2 more minutes.

PER SERVING:
    231 Calories; 12g Fat; 13g Protein; 21g Carbohydrate; 4g Dietary Fiber; trace Cholesterol; 798mg Sodium. Exchanges: ½ Grain (Starch); 2 Lean Meat; 2 Vegetable; 2 Fat; 0 Other Carbohydrates.

SERVING SUGGESTIONS: Serve on a bed of brown rice and a side of Asian Coleslaw (see page 254).

WARM BEAN SALAD

Serves 6

4 tablespoons olive oil
1 large onion, finely chopped
2 garlic cloves, pressed
1 large red bell pepper, seeded, deribbed, and cut into strips
5 ounces green beans
3 ounces mushrooms, cleaned and sliced
2 teaspoons dried thyme
2 tablespoons balsamic vinegar
2 (16-ounce) cans mixed beans
Chopped fresh parsley for garnish

In a skillet, heat 2 tablespoons of oil over medium heat. Add onion and cook for 2 minutes. Add garlic, red bell pepper, green beans, mushrooms, thyme, and vinegar. Cook for another 5 minutes, stirring occasionally.

Rinse and thoroughly drain mixed beans. Add beans with remaining oil to vegetables and stir until warmed through. Serve with chopped parsley sprinkled on top.

PER SERVING:
612 Calories; 11g Fat; 35g Protein; 98g Carbohydrate; 39g Dietary Fiber; 0mg Cholesterol; 24mg Sodium. Exchanges: 6 Grain (Starch); 2 Lean Meat; 1 Vegetable; 0 Fruit; 2 Fat.

SERVING SUGGESTIONS: Serve on a bed of cooked barley with a salad of baby greens.

Oats, Green Beans, and Barley Grow...

But the question is, how do you cook it? The barley, that is. Good question. It really depends on your barley. Do you have pearled barley or whole barley?

Pearled barley is lightly milled and slightly less nutritious and fibrous than its counterpart, whole barley. Cooking time is less, too. And lest you think pearled barley is akin to white rice, the endosperm of pearled barley is still very much in place, which means its cholesterol-blocking prowess remains intact. Good stuff!

Whole barley, also known as Scotch barley, on the other hand, has not only the endosperm but also the whole bran, leaving it with more than double the fiber of the pearled variety. It's used in commercial feed quite a bit, so you need to make sure you buy whole barley from a health food store and not a feed store! (Seriously, people do strange things to save money.) Whole barley should be soaked overnight to save on cooking time, but it still takes awhile to cook.

So first, let's take a look at pearled barley. Here is how you cook pearled barley (similar instructions are, most likely, on the bag or box that you bought it in):

The ratio is 1:3 barley to water. Bring a pot of water to a boil. Add the correct amount of pearled barley and allow it to return to a boil. Reduce the heat to low, cover, and cook 35 to 45 minutes, or until the barley is tender and the liquid completely absorbed. One cup of dried barley makes 3 cups cooked.

To cook whole barley (presoaked), the directions and ratios remain essentially the same, but the cooking time is a bit longer—about 1 hour. If you don't presoak, you're looking at at least 90 minutes of cooking time, maybe more.

But listen, barley was an important food in the ancient world. Greek athletes known for their athletic skills were big on barley. Gladiators in Rome were often called "barley eaters." So eat your barley and get burly. It worked in ancient times, it'll work now!

CREAM OF PEANUT SOUP

Serves 6

1 medium onion, chopped
2 celery stalks, chopped
2½ tablespoons butter
1¾ tablespoons flour
5 cups low-sodium vegetable broth
1¼ cups creamy peanut butter
1 cup half-and-half or light cream
14 peanuts, chopped
6 cilantro sprigs, chopped

In a large saucepan, sauté onion and celery in butter until soft, about 3 minutes. Stir in flour. Add broth; stir constantly and bring to a boil. Remove from heat.

Into a large bowl, strain broth, discarding the onion and celery. Add peanut butter and half-and-half; beat until thoroughly blended. Return to low heat to warm, but do not boil or cream will separate.

Garnish with chopped peanuts and cilantro.

PER SERVING:
507 Calories; 41g Fat; 25g Protein; 17g Carbohydrate; 7g Dietary Fiber; 39mg Cholesterol; 759mg Sodium. Exchanges: 1 Grain (Starch); 2½ Lean Meat; ½ Vegetable; 7 Fat; 0 Other Carbohydrates.

SERVING SUGGESTIONS: Serve soup with Blue Cheese Pasta Salad (see page 256) and crusty whole-grain bread.

HOPPIN' JOHN

Serves 6

1 tablespoon olive oil
1 cup chopped onion
2 garlic cloves, pressed
3 cups cooked brown rice
1 (16-ounce) can diced tomatoes
½ teaspoon dried basil
¼ tablespoon dried thyme
2 (16-ounce) cans black-eyed peas, rinsed and drained
½ cup chopped green onions
Salt and pepper to taste

In a large, deep skillet, heat olive oil over high heat. Sauté onion and garlic for 3 to 5 minutes, until onion is soft and slightly browned.

Add rice, tomatoes, basil, and thyme, stirring well, and cooking until heated through. Add black-eyed peas and stir.

Remove from heat. Stir in green onions and salt and pepper.

PER SERVING:
275 Calories; 4g Fat; 11g Protein; 50g Carbohydrate; 8g Dietary Fiber; 0mg Cholesterol; 567mg Sodium. Exchanges: 3 Grain (Starch); 1 Vegetable; ½ Fat.

SERVING SUGGESTIONS: Serve with a side of braised collard greens and a bowl of baby carrots on the table.

How You Bean?

If you notice, I use a great deal of canned beans in this book. Why? It's easier, that's why, and it's still inexpensive. Do you have to use canned beans? Not if you don't want to. You can easily make your own beans, save yourself some money, and feel like you've accomplished something all at the same time. Isn't that great?

Most cans of beans are about 15 ounces, which equals about 1½ cups of beans, depending on the size of the bean. Bigger beans will have a larger measurement. One pound of dried beans is equivalent to about 6 cups cooked beans, so keep that in mind when you're weighing and measuring, come bean time.

Here's how to get good beans when you're starting with dried ones:

- *Presoak first.* Presoaking will help your beans cook faster. Some people claim it will also cut out bean repercussions. I don't know that I agree with that, but I had to tell you anyway.
- *Salt not.* You have to wait until your beans are tender before adding salt. Salt can interrupt the tenderizing and then you're stuck with salty hard beans. Not good.
- *Water bottle.* You may need bottled water if your water is too hard. Hard water has too many minerals sometimes and the beans won't soften, no matter how long you cook them.
- *Age-old beans.* Old beans equals tough beans. Make sure you get fresh ones and that your grocery store turns over their stock. Pull from the back of the shelf, if you have to. Good grocery stores rotate their stock so the old ones will be in front.

The question I invariably get asked but hate to answer has to do with the "musicality" of the fine bean. There is no swift answer. If you ask enough people, they'll all come up with their own remedy for fixing this uncivilized problem. But the best answer to this question, believe it or not, is just to eat more beans. Oh yes, more beans. Then your body becomes bean acclimated and you'll be a little more discreet in the aftermath of your bean consumption. However, all bets are off that I'll ever show up at your house while you're going through the "adjustment" period!

SWEET-AND-SOUR CABBAGE

Serves 6

1 head green cabbage, shredded
2 onions, chopped
4 tart apples, pared and quartered
¼ cup apple juice
¼ cup lemon juice
1 tablespoon celery seed
3 tablespoons honey
⅛ teaspoon allspice
Salt and pepper to taste

In a slow cooker, combine all ingredients. Cook on high for 3 to 5 hours depending on how crunchy you want your cabbage.

PER SERVING:
137 Calories; 1g Fat; 3g Protein; 33g Carbohydrate; 6g Dietary Fiber; 0mg Cholesterol; 33mg Sodium. Exchanges: 0 Grain (Starch); 0 Lean Meat; 2 Vegetable; 1 Fruit; 0 Fat; ½ Other Carbohydrates.

SERVING SUGGESTIONS: Serve on a bed of whole wheat couscous and offer some baked sweet potatoes.

❄ Week Five

DAY ONE: Tortellini with Mushroom Sauce

DAY TWO: Tempeh Chili

DAY THREE: Black Bean and Cheese Melts

DAY FOUR: Minestrone Soup

DAY FIVE: Broccoli Stir-Fry

DAY SIX: Glazed Root Vegetable Medley

SHOPPING LIST

CONDIMENTS

Olive oil

Vegetable oil

Salsa, your choice

Honey

**Salad dressing, your choice (2 meals)

**Rice vinegar (1 meal)

**Mayonnaise (1 meal)

**Caesar salad dressing (1 meal)

**Toasted sesame oil (1 meal)

PRODUCE

12 ounces tempeh (found by the tofu in the produce area)

3 pounds yellow onions (keep on hand)

1 garlic head

1 bunch celery

18 ounces mushrooms

1 large zucchini

1 head green cabbage (only need ½, if your store sells halves)

1 medium spaghetti squash

1 bunch broccoli

2 medium parsnips

1 large turnip

1 bunch parsley

8 carrots

**Spinach (1 meal)

**Lettuce, not iceberg (1 meal)

**Salad toppings (2 meals)

**Green onions (1 meal)

**Coleslaw mix (2 meals)

**Baby carrots (1 meal)

**Romaine lettuce (1 meal)

**Cilantro (1 meal)

CANNED GOODS

2 (14.5-ounce) cans low-sodium vegetable broth

1 (14.5-ounce) can diced tomatoes

2 (15-ounce) cans black beans

1 (15.5-ounce) can kidney beans

2 (4.5-ounce) cans mild green chilies

1 (28-ounce) can tomato sauce

SPICES AND DRIED HERBS

Tarragon

Basil

Oregano

Sage

Rosemary

Thyme

Cumin

Chili powder

Cayenne pepper

Sesame seeds

DAIRY/DAIRY CASE

Butter

Cheese-filled tortellini (2 9-ounce packages)

Heavy cream (1½ cups)

Grated Parmesan cheese (¾ cup) **additional (1 meal)

Shredded Monterey Jack cheese (3 cups)

**Shredded Cheddar cheese (1 meal)

DRY GOODS

Elbow macaroni (1½ cups)

Brown rice (2 cups); **additional (1 meal)

**Croutons

**Dry-roasted peanuts

**Pearl barley (1 meal)

BREADS/BAKERY

6 Italian rolls

**Garlic bread (1 meal)

**Corn muffins (2 meals)

**Whole-grain rolls (1 meal)

FROZEN FOODS

1 (10-ounce) package green beans

OTHER

Aluminum foil

TORTELLINI WITH
MUSHROOM SAUCE

Serves 6

2 (9-ounce) packages cheese-filled tortellini
1½ tablespoons olive oil
2 garlic cloves, pressed
1½ teaspoons dried tarragon
6 ounces mushrooms, cleaned and sliced
1½ cups heavy cream
4½ tablespoons grated Parmesan cheese
Salt and pepper to taste

Prepare tortellini according to package directions until al dente; drain well and return to pan to keep warm.

In a skillet, heat oil over medium heat. Add garlic and tarragon and cook for 1 minute; add mushrooms and cook an additional 3 minutes. Pour in cream and stir thoroughly; bring to a boil and simmer for 3 minutes, stirring occasionally.

Add Parmesan cheese and salt and pepper, and stir well. Add sauce to the tortellini and mix well.

PER SERVING:
434 Calories; 24g Fat; 16g Protein; 38g Carbohydrate; 2g Dietary Fiber; 113mg Cholesterol; 422mg Sodium. Exchanges: 2 Grain (Starch); 1 Lean Meat; ½ Vegetable; 4 Fat.

SERVING SUGGESTIONS: Serve with a big spinach salad and garlic bread.

The Joy of Soy

Let's see, there's tofu, tempeh, TVP crumbles (texturized vegetable protein), miso, and soy milk. But for our purposes (and considering the soy products we have in this book), let's look at the first three:

- *Tofu:* What you have here is basically coagulated soy milk. I know that sounds icky, but that's what it is. You can purchase different types of tofu, which all correspond with what you want to do with it in the first place. You can even drain it, press it, and wear it, if you want to…this stuff is pretty darn flexible when it comes to what you can do with it. But let's say for the purpose of illustration you want to use it as a stand-in for ricotta cheese in a lasagna. Go with a firm or extra-firm tofu—less water and heartier for this job. Mix it with a little egg or water and ta da—tofu ricotta! This stuff is amazing.
- *TVP crumbles* (aka texturized vegetable protein): This soy product is an amazing substitute for ground beef or other meat. Its meaty countenance can even fool a meat eater. Comes either dried (easily reconstituted with water) or frozen, and adds texture and extra protein to a dish. Figure about 1 cup of dried TVP is equal to about 1 pound of meat if you're trying to use an old recipe and substitute TVP for the meat. About 1:1 hot water and TVP to reconstitute it—it is a very easy food to work with.
- *Tempeh:* This is a heartier type of fermented soybeans, or grains such as rice or wheat, made into flat blocks that can be sliced. Tempeh holds up well to nearly any cooking, including the barbecue and, naturally, stir-fries.

TEMPEH CHILI

Serves 6

    3 tablespoons vegetable oil
    12 ounces tempeh, cut into small cubes
    2 medium onions, chopped
    3 garlic cloves, pressed
    1 (28-ounce) can tomato sauce
    3–4 tablespoons chili powder
    3 teaspoons cumin
    3 teaspoons dried basil
    Salt and pepper to taste
    Cayenne to taste
    4 cups cooked brown rice

In a skillet, sauté tempeh until lightly browned, about 2 to 3 minutes. Add remainder of ingredients (except rice) and simmer for 20 minutes. Serve over rice.

PER SERVING:
471 Calories; 14g Fat; 19g Protein; 73g Carbohydrate; 8g Dietary Fiber; 0mg Cholesterol; 866mg Sodium. Exchanges: 4 Grain (Starch); 1½ Lean Meat; 2 Vegetable; 2 Fat.

SERVING SUGGESTIONS: Sprinkle some shredded Cheddar cheese on top of your chili along with some chopped green onions and serve with a big basket of corn muffins and butter.

BLACK BEAN AND CHEESE MELTS

Serves 6

3 tablespoons olive oil
12 ounces fresh mushrooms, cleaned and sliced
1 large onion, chopped
2 garlic cloves, pressed
6 individual Italian rolls
2 (15-ounce) cans black beans, drained, rinsed, and lightly crushed
2 (4.5-ounce) cans chopped mild green chilies, drained
½ cup salsa
3 cups shredded Monterey Jack cheese

Preheat oven to 350 degrees F.

In a large skillet, heat oil over medium-high heat. Add mushrooms, onion, and garlic; cook, stirring occasionally, about 10 minutes.

Cut rolls in half horizontally; scoop out centers, leaving a ½-inch-thick shell; set aside.

In a medium bowl, combine black beans, green chilies, and salsa.

Sprinkle bottom half of each loaf with cheese. Using half the mushroom mixture, evenly distribute on each loaf over the cheese. Spread bean mixture over mushrooms; top with remaining mushrooms, then remaining cheese.

Gently press top of bread over filling; wrap each loaf tightly in aluminum foil. Bake until heated through and cheese has melted, about 15 minutes.

PER SERVING:
504 Calories; 27g Fat; 26g Protein; 39g Carbohydrate; 10g Dietary Fiber; 51mg Cholesterol; 983mg Sodium. Exchanges: 2 Grain (Starch); 2½ Lean Meat; 1 Vegetable; 4 Fat.

SERVING SUGGESTIONS: Serve with a side of Basic Coleslaw (see page 253) and a bowl of baby carrots.

MINESTRONE SOUP

Serves 6

3 tablespoons olive oil

2 medium onions, chopped

3 celery stalks, chopped

2 tablespoons chopped fresh parsley

1 (14.5-ounce) can tomatoes, diced

2 (14.5-ounce) cans low-sodium vegetable broth

4 cups water

2 carrots, sliced

Salt and pepper to taste

1/8 teaspoon dried sage

1/2 teaspoon dried basil

1/4 teaspoon dried oregano

1/4 teaspoon dried thyme

1/8 teaspoon dried rosemary

1 (15.5-ounce) can kidney beans, drained

1 large zucchini, sliced

1 (10-ounce) package frozen green beans

1/2 head green cabbage, shredded

1 1/2 cups elbow macaroni

6 tablespoons grated Parmesan cheese

In a large soup pot, heat oil over medium-high heat. Add onions, celery, and parsley; sauté until soft, about 3 to 5 minutes. Stir in tomatoes, vegetable broth, water, carrots, salt and pepper, sage, basil, oregano, thyme, and rosemary. Bring to a boil; reduce heat and simmer, covered, for 45 minutes. Add kidney beans, zucchini, green beans, cabbage, and macaroni; cook over low heat until pasta is cooked, stirring occasionally, about 6 to 8 minutes. Serve sprinkled with cheese on top.

PER SERVING:
310 Calories; 14g Fat; 14g Protein; 34g Carbohydrate; 8g Dietary Fiber; 4mg Cholesterol; 630mg Sodium. Exchanges: 1 Grain (Starch); 1 Lean Meat; 2½ Vegetable; 2½ Fat.

SERVING SUGGESTIONS: Serve with a Caesar Salad (page 256) and whole-grain rolls.

BROCCOLI STIR-FRY

Serves 6

1 medium spaghetti squash
½ cup water
1 tablespoon oil
1 bunch broccoli, chopped
1½ onions, sliced into rings
1½ carrots, thinly sliced
2 celery stalks, chopped
1½ tablespoons sesame seeds

Halve squash lengthwise; scoop out seeds. In a large baking dish, place squash, cut side down, and the water. Prick the skin all over with a fork. Bake at 350 degrees F. for 30 to 40 minutes.

During the last 10 minutes of baking, in a skillet or wok, stir-fry remaining ingredients over medium-high heat.

To serve, carefully rake stringy squash pulp from its shell, separating it into strands that look like spaghetti. Spoon veggies over the squash.

PER SERVING:
87 Calories; 4g Fat; 4g Protein; 12g Carbohydrate; 5g Dietary Fiber; 0mg Cholesterol; 50mg Sodium. Exchanges: 0 Grain (Starch); 0 Lean Meat; 2 Vegetable; ½ Fat

SERVING SUGGESTIONS: To make this dish more substantial, serve everything, including the spaghetti squash, over brown rice. Add Asian Coleslaw (see page 254) for a nicely rounded meal.

GLAZED ROOT VEGETABLE MEDLEY

Serves 6

1 teaspoon salt

1 cup water

2 medium parsnips, peeled and cut into 1-inch pieces

4 medium carrots, peeled and cut into 1-inch pieces

1 large turnip, peeled and cut into 1-inch pieces

¼ cup honey

3 tablespoons butter

1 tablespoon dried rosemary

Salt and pepper to taste

In a saucepan, dissolve the teaspoon of salt in the water. Add vegetables, bring to a low boil, and boil for 10 minutes. Drain, reserving ½ cup liquid.

Place vegetables in slow cooker and add the reserved liquid.

Stir in honey, butter, rosemary, salt, and pepper. Cover and cook on low for 3 hours.

PER SERVING:
200 Calories; 6g Fat; 2g Protein; 37g Carbohydrate; 6g Dietary Fiber; 16mg Cholesterol; 453mg Sodium. Exchanges: 1 Grain (Starch); 1 Vegetable; 1 Fat; 1 Other Carbohydrates.

SERVING SUGGESTIONS: Serve veggies on a bed of barley and add a green salad and corn muffins.

❄ Week Six

DAY ONE: Vegetable Linguine with Honey Peanut Sauce
DAY TWO: Honeyed Tofu Cutlets
DAY THREE: Mexican Red Beans and Rice
DAY FOUR: Beware of Greeks Bearing Pizza
DAY FIVE: Braised Butternut Squash and Hominy
DAY SIX: Midwestern Soup

SHOPPING LIST

CONDIMENTS

Olive oil

Vegetable oil

Balsamic vinegar

Soy sauce (low-sodium, if available)

Vegetarian Worcestershire sauce

Salsa, your favorite (1½ cups)

Honey

Peanut butter

**Salad dressing, your choice (4 meals)

**Vinaigrette

PRODUCE

3 pounds extra-firm tofu

3 pounds yellow onions (keep on hand)

1 bunch green onions

1 garlic head

4 large green bell peppers

12 ounces mushrooms

1 bag carrots

1 head broccoli; **additional (1 meal)

4 cups snow peas

2–3 tomatoes

**1 cucumber

1 large butternut squash; **additional (1 meal)

2–3 large russet potatoes

1 bunch parsley; **additional (garnish)

1 bunch cilantro

**Lettuce, not iceberg (2 meals)

**Baby greens (1 meal)

**Romaine lettuce (2 meals)

**Salad toppings (3 meals)

CANNED GOODS

3 (14.5-ounce) cans low-sodium vegetable broth

1 (14.5-ounce) can diced tomatoes

3 (15-ounce) cans red kidney beans

1 (6-ounce) can tomato paste

1 (15-ounce) can hominy

1 (9-ounce) can Kalamata olives

SPICES AND DRIED HERBS

Oregano

Marjoram

Paprika

Cumin

Garlic powder

Cayenne pepper

Crushed red pepper flakes

Chili powder

DAIRY/DAIRY CASE

Butter

Light sour cream (optional)

Grated low-fat Cheddar cheese (optional)

Feta cheese (9 ounces; *more for side salad, about 3 ounces)

DRY GOODS

Flour

Linguine (1 pound)

Brown rice (2¼ cups)

½ cup peanuts

**Egg noodles (1 meal)

BREADS/BAKERY

6 pita bread rounds, 6 inches in diameter

**Corn muffins (1 meal)

FROZEN FOODS

1 (16-ounce) package frozen corn kernels

VEGETABLE LINGUINE WITH HONEY PEANUT SAUCE

Serves 6

1 pound linguine pasta
½ cup peanut butter
¼ cup honey
¼ cup low-sodium soy sauce
2 tablespoons chopped cilantro
¼ teaspoon crushed red pepper flakes
3 tablespoons olive oil
4 cups broccoli florets
4 cups snow peas, cut in half diagonally
4 cups sliced carrots
½ cup chopped peanuts

Cook linguine according to package directions until al dente.

In a small bowl, combine peanut butter, honey, soy sauce, cilantro, and red pepper flakes; mix well and set aside.

Drain linguine well and transfer to a bowl. Drizzle peanut sauce over linguine and toss well. Keep warm.

Meanwhile, in a large skillet, heat olive oil over medium-high heat. Add broccoli, snow peas, and carrots. Cook for 3 to 5 minutes, stirring frequently, till veggies are fork-tender.

Serve over linguine and garnish with peanuts.

PER SERVING:
647 Calories; 26g Fat; 22g Protein; 87g Carbohydrate; 9g Dietary Fiber; 0mg Cholesterol; 555mg Sodium. Exchanges: 4 Grain (Starch); 1 Lean Meat; 3 Vegetable; 4 Fat; 1 Other Carbohydrates.

SERVING SUGGESTION: A big green salad is adequate for this rich meal.

HONEYED TOFU CUTLETS

3 pounds extra-firm tofu, cut crosswise into ¼-inch slices
3 tablespoons olive oil
6 tablespoons honey
6 tablespoons low-sodium soy sauce
6 tablespoons balsamic vinegar
6 green onions, sliced

Cut tofu crosswise into ¼-inch-thick slices. Blot cutlets with paper towels to absorb excess moisture.

In a small bowl, combine oil, honey, soy sauce, and vinegar. Mix well and slowly pour mixture into a large skillet. Arrange tofu cutlets in skillet, immediately turning once to coat both sides. Cook over moderately high heat until golden brown. Turn and cook other side until crisp, a total of 4 to 5 minutes. Remove cutlets to a platter and sprinkle with sliced green onions.

PER SERVING:
316 Calories; 16g Fat; 20g Protein; 28g Carbohydrate; 2g Dietary Fiber; 0mg Cholesterol; 611mg Sodium. Exchanges: 0 Grain (Starch); 3 Lean Meat; 1 Vegetable; 0 Fruit; 2 Fat; ½ Other Carbohydrates.

SERVING SUGGESTIONS: Serve with baked butternut squash, egg noodles tossed in butter and parsley, and steamed broccoli.

MEXICAN RED BEANS AND RICE

2¼ cups brown rice

3 tablespoons olive oil

3 large onions, finely chopped

1 large green bell pepper, seeded, deribbed, and sliced

1½ tablespoons chili powder

1 teaspoon cumin

1 teaspoon garlic powder

3 (15-ounce) cans red kidney beans, rinsed and drained

1½ cups salsa

½ cup water

Grated low-fat Cheddar cheese (optional)

Light sour cream (optional)

Cook rice according to package directions. Set aside and keep warm.

In a large skillet, heat olive oil over medium-high heat. Add onions and green bell pepper and sauté until tender, about 3 to 4 minutes. Add spices and cook 1 more minute; stirring constantly. Add beans, salsa, and water and cook about 5 more minutes.

Serve over brown rice with a sprinkling of cheese and a dollop of sour cream.

PER SERVING:
567 Calories; 11g Fat; 19g Protein; 100g Carbohydrate; 18g Dietary Fiber; 3mg Cholesterol; 1048mg Sodium. Exchanges: 6 Grain (Starch); ½ Lean Meat; 1½ Vegetable; 2 Fat; 0 Other Carbohydrates.

SERVING SUGGESTION: Add a big green salad—that's all you need!

BEWARE OF GREEKS BEARING PIZZA

6 pita bread rounds, 6 inches in diameter
9 ounces crumbled feta cheese
2 teaspoons dried oregano
1 large onion, sliced paper thin into rings
1 (9-ounce) can Kalamata olives, pitted and chopped
3 tablespoons olive oil

Preheat broiler.

On a metal baking sheet, lay out the pita rounds. Sprinkle each with feta cheese and oregano. Add onion rings and olives. Drizzle olive oil over the top.

Place baking sheet in middle of oven and broil 5 minutes or until cheese melts and edges are golden brown. Cut in half to serve.

PER SERVING:
458 Calories; 28g Fat; 12g Protein; 40g Carbohydrate; 2g Dietary Fiber; 38mg Cholesterol; 1474mg Sodium. Exchanges: 2 Grain (Starch); 1 Lean Meat; ½ Vegetable; 0 Fruit; 5 Fat.

SERVING SUGGESTIONS: Serve with a tasty Greek Salad (see page 256).

BRAISED BUTTERNUT SQUASH AND HOMINY

Serves 6

"Our favorite! Good the first time around. Just as good after leftovers were frozen and served reheated! Really liked all the flavors. A veggie delight!"   —MaryPat M.

> 1 tablespoon vegetable oil
> 2 onions, chopped
> 1 butternut squash, peeled, seeded, and cut into 1-inch chunks
> 1 green bell pepper, seeded, deribbed, and coarsely diced
> 2 teaspoons paprika
> ½ teaspoon cumin
> 1½ teaspoons flour
> Salt and pepper to taste
> Pinch of cayenne pepper
> 1 (15-ounce) can hominy
> 2½ cups water
> 3 tablespoons chopped fresh parsley
> 2 tablespoons tomato paste
> 2 garlic cloves, pressed

In a large skillet, heat oil over high heat. Add onions, squash, green pepper, paprika, and cumin. Cook about 10 minutes, until onions are translucent.

Add flour, salt and pepper, and cayenne pepper; cook, stirring, for 1 more minute.

Stir in hominy, water, parsley, tomato paste, and garlic. Bring to a boil, reduce heat to low, and cover. Simmer for 30 minutes, until squash is tender. Add a bit more water if veggies look dry.

PER SERVING:
230 Calories; 3g Fat; 5g Protein; 50g Carbohydrate; 8g Dietary Fiber; 0mg Cholesterol; 210mg Sodium. Exchanges: 2½ Grain (Starch); 0 Lean Meat; 1 Vegetable; ½ Fat.

SERVING SUGGESTION: Serve with a simple baby greens salad.

MIDWESTERN SOUP

3 (14.5-ounce) cans low-sodium vegetable broth

1½ cups sliced carrots

1½ cups chopped onions

1½ cups frozen corn kernels

3 cups diced potatoes

3 garlic cloves, pressed

1 (14.5-ounce) can diced tomatoes, with juice

2 tablespoons vegetarian Worcestershire sauce

1 teaspoon dried marjoram

1 teaspoon dried oregano

Salt and pepper to taste

2 tablespoons butter

12 ounces mushrooms, cleaned and sliced

1½ cups chopped green onions

1½ cups seeded, deribbed, and diced green bell peppers

In a slow cooker, combine broth, carrots, onions, corn, potatoes, garlic, tomatoes, Worcestershire sauce, and herbs and spices. Cook on low for 6 to 8 hours.

Before serving, prepare garnishes. In a skillet, melt butter over medium-high heat. Add mushrooms and sauté till tender, about 3 to 4 minutes. Transfer to bowl and keep warm. Chop other veggies and put into individual small bowls for garnish.

Serve soup in bowls, allowing folks to add garnishes of their choice.

PER SERVING:
286 Calories; 8g Fat; 17g Protein; 40g Carbohydrate; 8g Dietary Fiber; 152mg Cholesterol; 473mg Sodium. Exchanges: 1½ Grain (Starch); 1½ Lean Meat; 3 Vegetable; 1 Fat; 0 Other Carbohydrates.

SERVING SUGGESTIONS: Serve with corn muffins and a hearty romaine lettuce salad.

SPRING

✿ Week One

DAY ONE: Delectable Bowties

DAY TWO: Broccoli Tofu Divan

DAY THREE: Lentil Tacos

DAY FOUR: Spinach Salad

DAY FIVE: Quinoa Salad

DAY SIX: Hot Crock Conglomerk

SHOPPING LIST

CONDIMENTS

Olive oil

Balsamic vinegar

Sherry (or use red grape juice)

Red grape juice (if not using sherry)

Salsa, your favorite (1½ cups); **additional (2 meals)

Prepared mustard

Tabasco sauce

12 sun-dried tomatoes, oil packed

**Salad dressing, your favorite (3 meals)

PRODUCE

1 (14–16-ounce) package firm tofu

3 pounds yellow onions (keep on hand)

Red onions (1 large, 2 small)

1 garlic head

1 large red bell pepper

1 small green bell pepper

1 bunch celery

2 carrots

1 large cucumber

8 plum tomatoes

3–4 tomatoes

1–2 heads lettuce

1 bunch red leaf lettuce (6 leaves)

18 ounces baby spinach; **additional (1 meal)

2 lemons

2 oranges (for juice and rind)

2 bunches arugula

1 bunch parsley

1 bunch basil

**Baby greens (1 meal)

**Salad toppings (3 meals)

**Sugar snap peas (1 meal)

**Baby carrots (2 meals)

CANNED GOODS

1 (28-ounce) can diced tomatoes

3 (14.5-ounce) cans low-sodium vegetable broth

2 (16-ounce) cans black beans

1 (16-ounce) can red kidney beans

1 (8-ounce) can low-sodium tomato sauce

2 (11-ounce) cans mandarin oranges in water

SPICES AND DRIED HERBS

Oregano

Basil

Cumin

Chili powder

DAIRY/DAIRY CASE

Butter

Skim milk (1 quart)

Sour cream (3 tablespoons)

Grated Romano cheese (optional garnish)

Shredded Cheddar cheese (2½ cups);

Grated Parmesan cheese (2 tablespoons)

**Blend of Shredded Cheddar-Jack cheese (1 meal)

DRY GOODS

Flour

Sugar

Brown rice (⅓ cup); **additional (1 meal)

Quinoa (1½ cups)

Millet (¼ cup)

Barley (¼ cup)

Red lentils (1 cup)

Bread crumbs (5 tablespoons)

Pine nuts (5 tablespoons)

Pecan halves (¾ cup)

Bowtie pasta (1 pound)

**Hummus (or make your own, page 259; 1 meal)

BREADS/BAKERY

12 corn tortillas

**Garlic bread (1 meal)

**Tortillas (1 meal)

**Pita bread (1 meal)

**Whole-grain rolls (1 meal)

FROZEN FOODS

1 (16-ounce) package broccoli spears

1 (16-ounce) package corn kernels

DELECTABLE BOWTIES

Serves 6

"Recipe Rating—10!!!! This was our favorite, by far, of all six recipes we tested. It is definitely a RAVE!! I will use this as a salad to bring to a potluck or picnic; it will be something different from your standard potato or macaroni salad. It is nice and light for the summer, too!"

—Marybeth M.

1 pound bowtie pasta
12 sun-dried tomatoes, oil packed, drained and cut into strips
8 plum tomatoes, chopped
2 bunches arugula, torn into bite-size pieces (more or less to taste)
8 sprigs fresh parsley, coarsely chopped
¾ bunch fresh basil, coarsely chopped
½ cup olive oil
2 large lemons, squeezed for juice
Salt and pepper to taste
Romano cheese (optional)

Cook pasta according to package directions until al dente. Drain and keep warm.

Meanwhile, in a large bowl, combine sun-dried tomatoes, plum tomatoes, arugula, parsley, and basil. Add pasta and toss.

Drizzle pasta with olive oil and lemon juice. Season with salt and pepper. Toss to mix well. Garnish with Romano cheese, if desired.

PER SERVING:
209 Calories; 19g Fat; 3g Protein; 11g Carbohydrate; 4g Dietary Fiber; 0mg Cholesterol; 53mg Sodium. Exchanges: 1½ Vegetable; 0 Fruit; 3½ Fat.

SERVING SUGGESTIONS: Serve with a salad of baby greens and garlic bread.

BROCCOLI TOFU DIVAN

Serves 6

1 (16-ounce) package frozen broccoli spears
1 (14–16-ounce) package firm tofu, drained and cut into ½-inch
    cubes
4½ tablespoons flour
3 cups skim milk
3 tablespoons butter
½ cup shredded Cheddar cheese
3 teaspoons prepared mustard
1 large onion, chopped
Salt and pepper to taste
1½ tablespoons sherry or red grape juice
5 tablespoons bread crumbs
2 tablespoons grated Parmesan cheese

Preheat oven to 375 degrees F. Lightly grease a 9-inch pie pan.

Cook broccoli according to package directions. Drain well. Cut into 3-inch pieces and arrange in prepared pan. Place tofu between paper towels and gently squeeze out excess water. Put tofu on top of broccoli.

Put flour in a small bowl and add a few tablespoons of milk, making a paste. Gradually add remaining milk, stirring.

In a small saucepan, melt butter over medium heat. Add milk mixture. Cook, stirring constantly, until mixture comes to full boil. Remove from heat and stir in cheese, mustard, onion, salt and pepper, and sherry. Evenly spoon sauce over broccoli and tofu.

In a small bowl, combine bread crumbs and Parmesan cheese and sprinkle over top of broccoli-tofu mixture. Bake, uncovered, for 25 minutes. Let stand 5 minutes before serving.

PER SERVING:
255 Calories; 13g Fat; 15g Protein; 19g Carbohydrate; 1g Dietary Fiber; 29mg Cholesterol; 298mg Sodium. Exchanges: ½ Grain (Starch); 2 Lean Meat; ½ Vegetable; ½ Non-Fat Milk; 2 Fat; 0 Other Carbohydrates.

SERVING SUGGESTIONS: Serve with brown rice, sautéed sugar snap peas, and steamed baby carrots.

LENTIL TACOS

Serves 6

"By far the favorite!! I took it to work and it was scarfed up by one and all from ages twenty to eighty!! Will make again!"   —Kathi S.

2 tablespoons olive oil
1 cup finely chopped onion
½ cup finely chopped celery
2 garlic cloves, pressed
1 cup red lentils
1 tablespoon chili powder
2 teaspoons cumin
2 cups low-sodium vegetable broth
1½ cups salsa
12 corn tortillas
2 cups shredded lettuce
2 cups chopped tomatoes
2 cups shredded Cheddar cheese
3 tablespoons sour cream

Preheat oven to 325 degrees F.

In a large skillet, heat oil over medium heat. Add onion, celery, and garlic and sauté for 5 minutes. Stir in lentils, chili powder, and cumin. Cook for 1 minute. Add broth, cover, and cook for 15 minutes or till lentils are tender.

Remove lid and cook about 10 minutes longer, stirring often till lentils are thickened. Stir in salsa.

Divide lentil mixture among tortillas and top with lettuce, tomatoes, cheese, and sour cream.

PER SERVING:
478 Calories; 21g Fat; 24g Protein; 51g Carbohydrate; 15g Dietary Fiber; 44mg Cholesterol; 1135mg Sodium. Exchanges: 2½ Grain (Starch); 2 Lean Meat; 2 Vegetable; 0 Non-Fat Milk; 3½ Fat.

SERVING SUGGESTIONS: Serve with a big green salad and set a bowl of baby carrots on the table.

SPINACH SALAD

4½ tablespoons olive oil

¾ cup pecan halves

¼ cup balsamic vinegar

4 teaspoons sugar

Salt and pepper to taste

18 ounces baby spinach leaves, washed and dried

2 (16-ounce) cans black beans, drained and rinsed

2 (11-ounce) cans mandarin oranges in water, drained

2 small red onions, thinly sliced

In a large skillet, heat oil over medium heat. Add pecans and cook about 3 minutes, till golden. Remove skillet from heat, and using a slotted spoon, transfer pecans to a plate.

To the oil in skillet add vinegar, sugar, and salt and pepper. Stir till sugar is dissolved. Remove skillet from heat.

In a large salad bowl, combine spinach, beans, oranges, and red onions. Pour dressing over the salad and toss well. Sprinkle the pecans on top.

PER SERVING:
413 Calories; 21g Fat; 15g Protein; 44g Carbohydrate; 13g Dietary Fiber; 0mg Cholesterol; 526mg Sodium. Exchanges: 1½ Grain (Starch); 1 Lean Meat; 1 Vegetable; ½ Fruit; 3½ Fat; 0 Other Carbohydrates.

SERVING SUGGESTION: Serve with Tex-Mex Quesadillas (see page 258).

Quinoa, Ancient Grain Wonder

Quinoa (pronounced KEEN-wah) is an ancient grain with a delicious nutty flavor that works well for many things, including the main-course salad featured here. It's also extremely nutritious and higher in protein than any other grain: a full 5 grams per ¼ cup (dry). Not only that, but the fiber content (3 grams) helps to up your fiber quota for the day.

The only preparation you need to know about ahead of time is the importance of rinsing it. The outside of the grain has a powdery residue on it that can be bitter, so rinsing it thoroughly (I'd do it more than once) is essential to getting a good result!

QUINOA SALAD

Serves 6

1½ cups quinoa

3 cups low-sodium vegetable broth

1 large red onion, finely chopped

1 large red bell pepper, cored, seeded, and chopped

1 large cucumber, peeled and chopped

½ cup chopped fresh basil leaves

¼ cup orange juice

1 tablespoon balsamic vinegar

1 teaspoon grated orange rind

Salt and pepper to taste

2 tablespoons olive oil

6 red leaf lettuce leaves

5 tablespoons pine nuts, toasted

In a colander, rinse quinoa thoroughly and drain. In a medium saucepan, bring broth to a boil, stir in quinoa, and return to a boil. Lower heat and simmer, covered, for 20 to 25 minutes, till liquid is absorbed. Let stand for 5 minutes.

In a large bowl, combine quinoa, red onion, red bell pepper, cucumber, and basil.

In a small bowl, combine orange juice, vinegar, orange rind, and salt and pepper. Whisk in oil. Pour dressing over quinoa and toss well. Arrange each serving on lettuce and garnish with pine nuts.

PER SERVING:
295 Calories; 10g Fat; 15g Protein; 40g Carbohydrate; 7g Dietary Fiber; 0mg Cholesterol; 276mg Sodium. Exchanges: 2 Grain (Starch); 1 Lean Meat; 1½ Vegetable; 0 Fruit; 1½ Fat.

SERVING SUGGESTIONS: Serve with pita bread triangles and Hummus for dipping (see page 259).

HOT CROCK CONGLOMERK

Serves 6

¼ cup millet
¼ cup barley
⅓ cup brown rice
1 large onion, chopped
1 small green bell pepper, cored, seeded, and chopped
2 garlic cloves, pressed
2 carrots, sliced
1 (16-ounce) can red kidney beans, rinsed and drained
1 (8-ounce) can low-sodium tomato sauce
1 (28 ounce) can diced tomatoes, drained, juice reserved
1½ cups frozen corn, thawed
1 teaspoon dried oregano
1 teaspoon dried basil
Salt and pepper to taste
2 cups water
Tabasco sauce to taste (optional)

In a slow cooker, combine all ingredients except reserved tomato juice and tabasco. Add water to reserved juice to equal 2½ cups. Stir into grain mixture. Cover and cook on low for 8 hours. Stir well before serving.

Ladle into bowls and season with a few drops of Tabasco or skip if you don't like spicy.

PER SERVING:
259 Calories; 2g Fat; 11g Protein; 53g Carbohydrate; 11g Dietary Fiber; 0mg Cholesterol; 480mg Sodium. Exchanges: 2½ Grain (Starch); 0 Lean Meat; 2½ Vegetable; 0 Fat.

SERVING SUGGESTIONS: Serve with a big spinach salad and whole-grain rolls.

🌹 Week Two

DAY ONE: Dilly Pasta

DAY TWO: Stir-Fried Rice with Tofu

DAY THREE: Lima Loaf

DAY FOUR: Lemony Lentil Salad

DAY FIVE: Bok Choy Stir-Fry

DAY SIX: Peppery Ziti with Fennel

SHOPPING LIST

CONDIMENTS

Olive oil

Mayonnaise

Dijon mustard

Sweet and sour stir-fry sauce (½ cup)

Soy sauce, low-sodium if available

Pitted green olives (15)

**Salad dressing, your choice (3 meals)

PRODUCE

1 (14–16-ounce) package firm tofu

3 pounds yellow onions (keep on hand)

1 red onion

1 bunch green onions

1 garlic head; **additional (2 meals)

4 red bell peppers

3 carrots

2 pounds baby bok choy

1 bunch broccoli; **additional (1 meal)

1½ cups snow peas

1 cucumber

2 fennel bulbs

3–4 lemons (for ⅓ cup juice)

1-inch piece ginger root

1 bunch basil

**Romaine lettuce (1 meal)

**Baby greens (1 meal)

**Lettuce, not iceberg (1 meal)

**Spinach (1 meal)

**Salad toppings (3 meals)

**Baby carrots (2 meals)

**Sweet potatoes (1 meal)

**Artichokes (1 meal)

CANNED GOODS

1 (14.5-ounce) can low-sodium vegetable broth

1 (28-ounce) can diced tomatoes

2 (4-ounce) cans mushroom pieces

1–2 jars roasted red bell peppers (need 1½ cups)

SPICES AND DRIED HERBS

Dillweed

Garlic powder

Tarragon

Crushed red pepper flakes

Sesame seeds

**Cinnamon

DAIRY/DAIRY CASE

Eggs (3)

Skim milk (½ cup)

Plain nonfat yogurt (1¼ cups)

Grated Parmesan cheese (2¼ cups)

Shredded Cheddar cheese (½ cup)

**Butter (1 meal)

DRY GOODS

Sugar (½ cup)

Cornstarch

Nonfat dry milk (1 cup)

Penne pasta (12 ounces)

Ziti pasta (1 pound)

Brown rice (5¼ cups)

Lentils (1 pound)

BREADS/BAKERY

3 slices whole wheat bread

**Garlic bread (2 meals)

**Whole-grain rolls (1 meal)

FROZEN FOODS

1 (16-ounce) package frozen peas

1 (15-ounce) bag frozen lima beans

DILLY PASTA

For optimal flavor, make this pasta salad ahead of time so you can let it chill for several hours.

1½ cups snow peas, cut into ½-inch pieces
3 cups chopped broccoli florets
12 ounces penne pasta
1¼ cups plain nonfat yogurt
½ cup skim milk
1 tablespoon mayonnaise
5 tablespoons grated Parmesan cheese
2 teaspoons Dijon mustard
¾ teaspoon dillweed
½ teaspoon garlic powder
15 small pitted green olives, chopped
2 small onions, cut into rings

Place snow peas and broccoli in a colander. Cook penne pasta according to package directions until al dente. Pour pasta and cooking water over vegetables in colander, slightly cooking veggies. Rinse under cold water and drain.

In a large bowl, combine remaining ingredients, mixing well. Add pasta and veggies. Mix well. Chill several hours, if possible, to blend flavors.

PER SERVING:
326 Calories; 5g Fat; 14g Protein; 55g Carbohydrate; 4g Dietary Fiber; 5mg Cholesterol; 258mg Sodium. Exchanges: 2½ Grain (Starch); 0 Lean Meat; 1 Vegetable; 0 Fruit; ½ Non-Fat Milk; ½ Fat; 0 Other Carbohydrates.

SERVING SUGGESTIONS: Serve with a romaine salad and some garlic bread.

STIR-FRIED RICE WITH TOFU

Serves 6

2 tablespoons olive oil

6 green onions, diagonally sliced

3 red bell peppers, seeded, deribbed, and thinly sliced

3 garlic cloves, pressed

3 small carrots, thinly sliced

4½ cups cooked brown rice

1 (16-ounce) package frozen peas (use baby peas or petite peas for better flavor)

1 (14–16-ounce) package firm tofu, drained and cubed

½ cup sweet and sour stir-fry sauce

3 tablespoons low-sodium soy sauce

In a large skillet, heat oil over high heat. Add green onions, peppers, garlic, and carrots and cook, stirring, for 2 minutes. Add rice and peas, and cook for 5 minutes, stirring often, till rice is heated through.

Add tofu, stir-fry sauce, and soy sauce to rice mixture. Stirring gently for about 1 minute, cook till heated through.

PER SERVING:
383 Calories; 10g Fat; 16g Protein; 61g Carbohydrate; 9g Dietary Fiber; 0mg Cholesterol; 1115mg Sodium. Exchanges: 3½ Grain (Starch); 1½ Lean Meat; 2 Vegetable; 1½ Fat.

SERVING SUGGESTION:S Serve with a salad of baby greens and set a bowl of baby carrots on the table.

LIMA LOAF

3 eggs, beaten
1 cup nonfat dry milk
¾ cup water
3 slices whole wheat bread, crumbled
½ cup shredded Cheddar cheese
⅓ cup grated Parmesan cheese
1 tablespoon dried tarragon
Salt and pepper to taste
1 (15-ounce) bag frozen lima beans, thawed
¾ cup finely chopped onion
2 (4-ounce) cans mushroom pieces, drained

Preheat oven to 325 degrees F. Grease a 5 × 9-inch loaf pan.

In a large bowl, combine eggs, dry milk, water, bread, cheeses, tarragon, and salt and pepper. Mix well. Add remaining ingredients and mix till blended.

Pack into loaf pan and bake for 45 minutes, till set.

PER SERVING:
345 Calories; 11g Fat; 26g Protein; 36g Carbohydrate; 7g Dietary Fiber; 132mg Cholesterol; 485mg Sodium. Exchanges: 1½ Grain (Starch); 2 Lean Meat; ½ Vegetable; 1 Non-Fat Milk; 1 Fat.

SERVING SUGGESTIONS: Serve with Sweet Potato Fries (see page 258) and steamed broccoli.

DO AHEAD TIP: Cook lentils for tomorrow night's meal.

LEMONY LENTIL SALAD

⅓ cup lemon juice

⅓ cup chopped fresh basil

2 teaspoons Dijon mustard

Salt and pepper to taste

⅓ cup olive oil

4 cups cooked lentils

1 cup grated Parmesan cheese

1 medium red bell pepper, seeded, deribbed, and chopped

1 cup peeled and chopped cucumber

½ cup finely chopped red onion

In a large bowl, whisk together lemon juice, basil, mustard, and salt and pepper. Gradually add oil. Add lentils, cheese, bell pepper, cucumber, and red onion. Toss to coat.

PER SERVING:
338 Calories; 17g Fat; 18g Protein; 31g Carbohydrate; 11g Dietary Fiber; 10mg Cholesterol; 273mg Sodium. Exchanges: 1½ Grain (Starch); 1½ Lean Meat; ½ Vegetable; 0 Fruit; 2½ Fat; 0 Other Carbohydrates.

SERVING SUGGESTIONS: Serve with whole-grain rolls, butter, and sautéed spinach.

BOK CHOY STIR-FRY

3 tablespoons olive oil

2 garlic cloves, pressed

2 teaspoons peeled and grated ginger root

½ teaspoon crushed red pepper flakes

2 pounds baby bok choy, cleaned and cut into bite-size pieces

⅓ cup low-sodium vegetable broth

3 tablespoons low-sodium soy sauce

1½ teaspoons sugar

1 teaspoon cornstarch

2 teaspoons sesame seeds

6 cups cooked brown rice

In a large skillet, heat oil over medium-high heat and swirl to coat pan. Add garlic, ginger, and red pepper flakes, cooking about 30 seconds.

Add bok choy and cook for 3 minutes, stirring often. Stir in broth, soy sauce, sugar, and cornstarch and bring to a boil, stirring constantly. Cook until thickened, about 1 minute. Remove from heat and sprinkle with sesame seeds.

Serve over brown rice.

PER SERVING:
317 Calories; 9g Fat; 8g Protein; 52g Carbohydrate; 5g Dietary Fiber; 0mg Cholesterol; 429mg Sodium. Exchanges: 3 Grain (Starch); 0 Lean Meat; 1 Vegetable; 1½ Fat; 0 Other Carbohydrates.

SERVING SUGGESTIONS: Serve with steamed artichokes, baby carrots, and mayo for dipping.

A Bok Choy Haiku

A friendly cabbage
On the stovetop cooking
In stir-fries and sides.

Okay, so I'm no poet and my haiku isn't going to be published anytime soon. I do, however, want to pay homage to this wonderful vegetable. A mere 10 calories for about ½ cup of this awesome veggie is one of the main draws for dieters. For nondieters and people interested in good nutrition, it's a good source of calcium and vitamin C.

Bok choy is flavorful and adds a nice crunch to any stir-fry. The green leaves should be separated from the big white stalks, as the leaves take very little time to cook and the white takes a little longer. Baby bok choy is also delicious and wonderful and easy as a side dish. Highly recommended in Asian dishes and nonethnic dishes alike.

PEPPERY ZITI WITH FENNEL

1 pound ziti pasta

1 tablespoon olive oil

2 fennel bulbs, base and leafy stems discarded, bulb thinly sliced

1 large onion, finely chopped

3 garlic cloves, pressed

Salt and pepper to taste

1 (28-ounce) can diced tomatoes, with juice

½ cup grated Parmesan cheese

1½ cups roasted red bell peppers, jarred variety, packed in oil

Cook pasta according to package directions until al dente. Drain and set aside.

In a skillet, heat oil over medium heat. Add fennel and onion, and cook, stirring, till fennel is soft, about 6 minutes. Add garlic and salt and pepper and cook for an additional minute. Add tomatoes and bring to a boil. Transfer to slow cooker. Add cooked ziti and stir to combine. Sprinkle Parmesan cheese over top.

Cover and cook on low for 4 hours or on high for 2 hours, till hot and bubbly. Garnish with red roasted peppers.

PER SERVING:
305 Calories; 5g Fat; 12g Protein; 55g Carbohydrate; 6g Dietary Fiber; 5mg Cholesterol; 365mg Sodium. Exchanges: 3 Grain (Starch); ½ Lean Meat; 1½ Vegetable; ½ Fat.

SERVING SUGGESTIONS: A big green salad and garlic bread will do the trick.

🌹 Week Three

DAY ONE: Spaghetti with Rice 'n Grain Balls

DAY TWO: "Just Peachy" Tofu

DAY THREE: Minty Couscous Salad

DAY FOUR: Grilled Cheese with Avocado and
Sun-Dried Tomatoes

DAY FIVE: Beety Barley Pilaf

DAY SIX: Cashew Lentil Loaf

SHOPPING LIST

CONDIMENTS

Olive oil

Dijon mustard

French salad dressing

Peach jam

**Salsa, your favorite (try chipotle salsa!)

**Salad dressing, your choice (2 meals)

**Soy sauce, low-sodium if available (1 meal)

PRODUCE

2 (14–16-ounce) packages firm tofu

3 pounds yellow onions (keep on hand); **additional

1 bunch green onions

1 garlic head; **additional (1 meal)

1 red bell pepper

1 green chili pepper

1 bunch celery; **additional (1 meal)

6 carrots

3 tomatoes; **additional 3 tomatoes

1 bunch watercress

9 lemons (for 1⅛ cups juice)

1 bunch parsley

1 bunch mint

1 bunch dill

**Spinach leaves (2 meals)

**Salad toppings (2 meals)

**Bok choy (1 meal)

**Sugar snap peas (1 meal)

**Grape tomatoes (1 meal)

**Baby carrots (2 meals)

**Cucumber (1 meal)

**Russet potatoes (1 meal)

**Broccoli (1 meal)

**1 ripe avocado

CANNED GOODS

3 (14.5-ounce) cans low-sodium vegetable broth

1 jar sun-dried tomatoes, in oil

2 (15-ounce) cans chickpeas

1 (28-ounce) jar spaghetti sauce

1 (8-ounce) can tomato sauce

1 (16-ounce) jar pickled beets

SPICES AND DRIED HERBS

Italian seasoning

Garlic powder

Caraway seeds

DAIRY/DAIRY CASE

Butter

Eggs (3)

Plain nonfat yogurt (1 cup)

Grated Parmesan cheese (1½ cups)

Shredded Cheddar cheese (5 cups)

DRY GOODS

Whole wheat flour

Yellow cornmeal (3 ounces)

Sugar

Nonfat dry milk (⅓ cup)

Spaghetti (1 pound)

Brown rice (½ cup); **additional (1 meal)

Couscous (½ cups)

Pearl barley (2 cups)

Lentils (2 cups)

Golden raisins (½ cup)

Cashews (1 cup)

BREADS/BAKERY

12 slices whole-grain bread

**Whole-grain rolls (1 meal)

SPAGHETTI WITH RICE 'N GRAIN BALLS

Serves 6

½ cup yellow cornmeal
½ cup whole wheat flour
⅓ cup nonfat dry milk
¼ teaspoon garlic powder
1 teaspoon Italian seasoning
Salt and pepper to taste
1 cup cooked brown rice
½ cup tomato sauce
½ cup water
2 tablespoons finely minced onion
1 tablespoon olive oil
12 ounces spaghetti
1 (28-ounce) jar spaghetti sauce
1½ cups grated Parmesan cheese

Preheat oven to 375 degrees F. Grease a cookie sheet.

In a large bowl, combine cornmeal, flour, dry milk, garlic powder, Italian seasoning, and salt and pepper. Mix well. Stir in rice.

In a small bowl, combine tomato sauce, water, onion, and oil. Add to rice mixture, mixing well till all ingredients are moistened.

Form 24 walnut-size balls from the mixture and place on cookie sheet. Bake 20 minutes, till lightly browned.

Cook spaghetti according to package directions until al dente; drain and keep warm. In a large saucepan, warm spaghetti sauce. Combine sauce and rice balls and serve over spaghetti. Sprinkle with Parmesan cheese.

PER SERVING:
620 Calories; 16g Fat; 24g Protein; 95g Carbohydrate; 9g Dietary Fiber; 17mg Cholesterol; 1194mg Sodium. Exchanges: 4½ Grain (Starch); 1 Lean Meat; 4½ Vegetable; ½ Non-Fat Milk; 2½ Fat.

SERVING SUGGESTION: Serve with a big spinach salad—that's really all you need.

DO AHEAD TIP: Press tofu for 1 hour.

"JUST PEACHY" TOFU

1½ pounds firm tofu, cut into 1-inch-thick slices
½ cup French salad dressing
4 tablespoons peach jam
¼ cup finely chopped onion
½ cup golden raisins

Place tofu between two cookie sheets for 1 hour to squeeze out the water and flatten the tofu. Put something heavy on top (this book?) and slightly tilt the cookie sheets so the water will drain off.

Preheat oven to 350 degrees F. Lightly grease a 6 × 10-inch shallow baking dish.

Cut pressed tofu into 1-inch cubes and place in prepared dish.

Combine remaining ingredients and mix well. Pour over tofu cubes. Bake uncovered for 45 minutes.

Move baking dish closer to broiler element. Turn on broiler and broil for another 2 to 3 minutes, till crisp. Watch it carefully and don't let it burn.

PER SERVING:
253 Calories; 14g Fat; 10g Protein; 26g Carbohydrate; 2g Dietary Fiber; 3mg Cholesterol; 295mg Sodium. Exchanges: 1 Lean Meat; 0 Vegetable; 1 Fruit; 2 Fat; ½ Other Carbohydrates.

SERVING SUGGESTIONS: Serve with brown rice, sautéed bok choy, and sugar snap peas sautéed with a little garlic and some soy sauce.

DO AHEAD TIP: Prepare salad. Chill and serve cold.

MINTY COUSCOUS SALAD

Serves 6

1½ cups cooked couscous
1½ cups chopped tomatoes
1½ cups chopped green onions
1½ cups chopped fresh parsley
½ cup chopped celery
2¼ cups canned chickpeas, rinsed and drained
Salt and pepper to taste
¾ cup olive oil
1⅛ cups lemon juice
5 garlic cloves, pressed
3 teaspoons finely chopped fresh mint

Mix all ingredients and serve cold.

PER SERVING:
548 Calories; 29g Fat; 12g Protein; 64g Carbohydrate; 8g Dietary Fiber; 0mg Cholesterol; 299mg Sodium. Exchanges: 3½ Grain (Starch); 1 Vegetable; ½ Fruit; 5½ Fat.

SERVING SUGGESTION: This is a rich salad—serve with a relish tray of grape tomatoes, celery sticks, and baby carrots; that's really all you need.

DO AHEAD TIP: If you're following the Serving Suggestion for tomorrow night's meal, make the Simple Gazpacho so it can be well chilled.

GRILLED CHEESE WITH AVOCADO AND SUN-DRIED TOMATOES

Serves 6

"I would rate the recipe a 9. It's a wonderful grown-up version of a childhood favorite! The avocado and tomatoes added just enough extra flavor for my family to think this was a special meal, not an old staple."

—Catherine C.

12 slices whole-grain bread
3 tablespoons butter, at room temperature
2 cups shredded Cheddar cheese
4 tablespoons drained and sliced oil-packed sun-dried tomatoes
1 ripe avocado, cut in half, pitted, peeled, and each half cut into
*   6 slices*

Butter one side of each slice of bread. Preheat a large nonstick skillet over medium-low heat.

Place 3 tablespoons of cheese on six of the unbuttered sides of bread. Add 2 teaspoons of sun-dried tomato slices. Arrange two slices of avocado on top of the tomato slices. Sprinkle on another 2 teaspoons of cheese. Top each with a slice of bread, buttered side up.

In the heated skillet, cook sandwiches for 5 to 7 minutes per side, or until toasted and golden with the cheese melted.

PER SERVING:
473 Calories; 28g Fat; 18g Protein; 43g Carbohydrate; 7g Dietary Fiber; 55mg Cholesterol; 750mg Sodium. Exchanges: 2½ Grain (Starch); 1½ Lean Meat; 0 Fruit; 4½ Fat.

SERVING SUGGESTION: Serve with Simple Gazpacho: dice 3 large ripe tomatoes, 1 small onion, 1 small cucumber, and salt and pepper to taste. Now add enough of your favorite jarred salsa (I use a chipotle salsa that's wonderful) to "soup" it up. Chill for a few hours or overnight. Stir before serving.

BEETY BARLEY PILAF

1 tablespoon olive oil
1 large onion, finely chopped
2 cups pearl barley
1 (16-ounce) jar pickled beets, finely chopped, juice reserved
4 cups low-sodium vegetable broth
1 teaspoon sugar
Salt and pepper to taste
1 teaspoon Dijon mustard
1 bunch watercress, stems removed
¼ cup snipped fresh dill
1 cup plain nonfat yogurt

In a medium saucepan, heat oil over medium heat. Add onion and sauté till translucent, about 3 to 4 minutes. Stir in barley, beet juice (not the beets!), broth, sugar, salt, and pepper; bring to a boil. Lower heat, cover, and simmer for 25 minutes, till barley is just tender.

Stir in pickled beets and mustard; cover and cook for 5 minutes. Remove from heat and stir in watercress, dill, and yogurt. Cover and let stand for 5 minutes so the watercress can wilt.

PER SERVING:
444 Calories; 6g Fat; 14g Protein; 87g Carbohydrate; 14g Dietary Fiber; 2mg Cholesterol; 1332mg Sodium. Exchanges: 5½ Grain (Starch); 0 Lean Meat; ½ Vegetable; 0 Non-Fat Milk; 1 Fat; 0 Other Carbohydrates.

SERVING SUGGESTIONS: Serve with a big spinach salad and some whole-grain rolls.

DO AHEAD TIP: Cook lentils for tomorrow night's meal.

A Cook's Note from My Editor

Having an editor who is also an accomplished cook is quite a bonus if you're a cookbook author! Here are a couple of suggestions from Caroline's kitchen for speedy vegetarian meals that I know you're going to love.

The idea here is to go from pot to plate. (Faster cleanup, too.) The decision-making process goes something like this: Do I want Asian, Indian, Italian, Mediterranean, Middle Eastern, or Mexican? Do I want to eat with a fork, a spoon, or chopsticks? Do I want something more solid or soupy? Do I want it hot or cold? Do I have leftovers I want to use? Also, think in terms of substitutions: you do not *have* to have most of these ingredients. Then choose:

1. *Grain:* Whole wheat noodles or a fast-cooking grain like quinoa (which provides a complete protein) or bulgur wheat, or any leftover grain you have. I usually have some cooked barley in the fridge. You can add it to anything, and it even makes a good hot cereal.
2. *Protein:* Tempeh, tofu, beans, chickpeas, nuts, TVP—the idea is that you have it on hand and don't have to cook it.
3. *Vegetable:* Nearly anything will work here, though you have to keep in mind that a few vegetables, like eggplant, can require special attention and are easier to deal with as leftovers.

You start with a little oil and some garlic. You'll be adding liquid, herbs or spices, and the above ingredients. Keep it simple, but don't be afraid to try things. For instance, for an easy peanut sauce, I combine 2 tablespoons peanut butter, 2 tablespoons soy sauce, 4 tablespoons water, a mashed garlic clove, and a shake of cayenne pepper in a jar, and shake like mad. I pour that over cold noodles and shredded cucumber with a garnish of nuts or stir it all up in a pot with broccoli and tempeh. You can play around with this, using any nut butter (almond butter is nice with cumin) or tahini for a more traditional sesame paste. You can add or subtract liquid. You can throw cilantro on it. Once when I didn't have soy sauce I used curry powder with a little soy milk and ended up with a dish that was essentially Thai and really delicious.

For a more Italian version, use olive oil, garlic, basil, and pine nuts. You don't have to blend this into pesto sauce. Toss it with pasta with fresh tomatoes. Stir it up with green beans and quinoa. Don't have basil? Substitute any green herb you like. Don't have pine nuts? Try some other nut or seed. Parmesan is great on this, but don't be afraid to try other cheeses for variation. Mozzarella can be great if the tomatoes are fresh.

Want something more Mediterranean? Combine the grain and protein with garlic, oil, Kalamata olives, tomatoes, dried apricots, rosemary, and a dash of red wine vinegar. Top with feta cheese. If you have leftover eggplant, use it now, and don't forget the pepper.

Trying to use things up? Make curry. For this, most vegetables work but so do fruits and nuts: apples, bananas, dried fruit (that includes raisins), cheese, onions, nuts, and assorted leftovers. Frozen vegetables definitely work in this one. Peas, spinach, and corn make a nice trio here. For liquid you can use milk, soy milk, coconut milk, vegetable broth, or even tomato sauce. I usually use 1–2 tablespoons curry powder, 1–2 teaspoons garam masala, and a shake of red pepper flakes. Stir it all around in a pot and get creative with the condiments. All of the following have worked for me in a pinch: chutney, nuts, thick jams, mustard, orange slices, yogurt, shredded cheese, sliced mango. Shredded coconut would also go with this.

If you want to take the Middle Eastern route, thin some hummus with broth or oil. You may need to add more garlic or spices depending on what you started with.

A great summer supper is more Mexican: whole wheat noodles tossed with avocado, fresh tomato, oil, cilantro, garlic, and cheese. You don't even really need the garlic if the avocado and tomato are really good.

CASHEW LENTIL LOAF

Serves 6

1 tablespoon olive oil
1 large onion, finely chopped
2 celery stalks, chopped
2 cups shredded carrots
2 garlic cloves, pressed
1 red bell pepper, seeded, deribbed, and chopped
½ green chili pepper, diced
1 tablespoon caraway seeds
Salt and pepper to taste
2 cups lentils, cooked
3 cups shredded Cheddar cheese
1 cup coarsely chopped cashews
3 eggs, beaten

In a large skillet, heat oil over medium heat. Add onion and celery and cook, stirring, till celery softens, about 5 minutes. Add carrots, garlic, red bell pepper, chili pepper, caraway seeds, and salt and pepper and cook for about 2 minutes, stirring often. Remove from heat and set aside.

In a large mixing bowl, combine lentils, cheese, and cashews. Add carrot mixture and stir well. Add eggs, and mix till well blended. Spoon into greased loaf pan or casserole dish that fits into your slow cooker and cover tightly with aluminum foil.

Place in slow cooker and pour enough boiling water to come 1 inch up the sides. Cover and cook on high for 4 to 5 hours, till set.

PER SERVING:
525 Calories; 34g Fat; 28g Protein; 29g Carbohydrate; 9g Dietary Fiber; 165mg Cholesterol; 419mg Sodium. Exchanges: 1½ Grain (Starch); 3 Lean Meat; 1½ Vegetable; 5 Fat.

SERVING SUGGESTIONS: Serve with old-fashioned mashed potatoes, steamed broccoli, and steamed baby carrots.

 # Week Four

DAY ONE: Lemon Pepper Pasta

DAY TWO: Quinoa and Beans

DAY THREE: Tofu Spinach Lasagna

DAY FOUR: Italian Cabbage Soup

DAY FIVE: Hawaiian Sandwiches

DAY SIX: Lentil Sloppy Joes

SHOPPING LIST

CONDIMENTS

Olive oil

Balsamic vinegar

Ketchup

Prepared mustard

**Salad dressing (2 meals)

**Honey (1 meal)

**Mayonnaise (3 meals)

**Rice vinegar (3 meals)

**Italian salad dressing (1 meal)

**Olives (1 meal)

PRODUCE

1 (16-ounce) package firm tofu

3 pounds yellow onions (keep on hand)

2 garlic heads

3 large red bell peppers

2 large green bell peppers

1 large yellow bell pepper

1 bunch celery

2 large tomatoes

1 head savoy or green cabbage (savoy is sweeter)

2 lemons

1 bunch cilantro

**Lettuce, not iceberg (1 meal)

**Baby greens (1 meal)

**Salad toppings (2 meals)

**Coleslaw mix (2 meals)

**Carrots or 1 bag shredded (1 meal)

**Chopped veggies (clean out the crisper!)(1 meal)

CANNED GOODS

5 (14.5-ounce) cans low-sodium vegetable broth

2 (14-ounce) cans black-eyed peas

2 (15.5-ounce) cans cannellini beans (or use white beans)

1 (32-ounce) jar spaghetti sauce

1 (20-ounce) can pineapple tidbits

SPICES AND DRIED HERBS

Oregano

Basil

Thyme

Italian seasoning

Cumin

Cayenne pepper

Garlic powder

DAIRY/DAIRY CASE

Skim milk

Shredded Cheddar cheese (12 ounces)

Shredded mozzarella cheese (3 cups)

Grated Parmesan or Romano cheese (1 cup)

**Butter (3 meals)

**Grated cheese, your choice (1 meal)

DRY GOODS

Brown sugar

Fettuccine pasta (1 pound)

Lasagna noodles (8 ounces)

Quinoa (1½ cups)

Lentils (3 cups)

**Raisins (1 meal)

**Walnuts (1 meal)

**Pasta, your choice (1 meal)

BREADS/BAKERY

6 slices whole wheat country bread (½-inch thick) or buy a
   loaf and cut it yourself

12 slices whole wheat bread

6 whole-grain hamburger buns

**Corn muffins (2 meals)

**Corn bread (1 meal)

**Garlic bread (1 meal)

FROZEN FOODS

1 (10-ounce) package frozen chopped spinach

LEMON PEPPER PASTA

Serves 6

1 pound fettuccine pasta

3 tablespoons olive oil

2 large red bell peppers, cored, seeded, and cut into strips

1 large yellow bell pepper, cored, seeded, and cut into strips

1½ tablespoons lemon zest (see sidebar on zest, page 122)

Salt and pepper to taste

1½ cups skim milk

⅔ cup shredded Cheddar cheese

Cook pasta according to package directions until al dente. Drain.

In a large skillet, heat oil over medium-high heat. Add peppers. Cook, stirring often, for 5 minutes. Sprinkle with lemon zest and salt and pepper, and stir till blended.

Reduce heat to low. Add cooked pasta, milk, and cheese. Toss till pasta is heated through and cheese is melted.

PER SERVING:
423 Calories; 17g Fat; 17g Protein; 50g Carbohydrate; 2g Dietary Fiber; 31mg Cholesterol; 213mg Sodium. Exchanges: 3 Grain (Starch); 1 Lean Meat; ½ Vegetable; 0 Fruit; 0 Non-Fat Milk; 2½ Fat.

SERVING SUGGESTIONS: Serve with a big baby greens salad and corn muffins and honey butter.

DO AHEAD TIP: Make quinoa for tomorrow night's meal.

QUINOA AND BEANS

Serves 6

"Quinoa is yummy—who knew?"

—Abbe L.

1½ cups quinoa

3 cups low-sodium vegetable broth

1 teaspoon cumin

¼ teaspoon cayenne pepper

3 tablespoons olive oil

1 large red bell pepper, cored, seeded, and sliced

1 large green bell pepper, cored, seeded, and sliced

1 large onion, coarsely chopped

4 garlic cloves, pressed

2 (14-ounce) cans black-eyed peas, rinsed and drained

¾ cup chopped cilantro stems and leaves

Salt and pepper to taste

In a large saucepan, cook quinoa in the vegetable broth seasoned with cumin and cayenne pepper; bring to a boil, lower heat, and simmer, covered, for 10 minutes.

Meanwhile, in a skillet, heat oil over medium heat. Add red and green bell peppers, onion, and garlic. Cook, stirring often, for 5 minutes or till veggies are soft.

Add sautéed veggie mixture to cooked quinoa. Stir in black-eyed peas and cilantro. Season with salt and pepper. Simmer for about 5 minutes till heated through.

PER SERVING:
720 Calories; 11g Fat; 44g Protein; 116g Carbohydrate; 20g Dietary Fiber; 0mg Cholesterol; 299mg Sodium. Exchanges: 7½ Grain (Starch); 3 Lean Meat; 1 Vegetable; 2 Fat.

SERVING SUGGESTIONS: Serve with coleslaw and cornbread.

TOFU SPINACH LASAGNA

Serves 6

1 (8-ounce) package lasagna noodles

1½ cups water

1 (32-ounce) jar spaghetti sauce

1 pound firm tofu, softened

1 (10-ounce) package frozen chopped spinach, thawed and drained

2 teaspoons Italian seasoning

¼ tablespoon garlic powder

3 cups shredded mozzarella cheese

Preheat oven to 350 degrees F.

Cook lasagna noodles according to package directions until al dente; drain.

In a large bowl, combine water and sauce; set aside.

Slightly drain tofu, but do not squeeze out all the water. Place in a blender container and blend until smooth. In a large bowl, combine smooth tofu, spinach, seasoning, garlic powder, and 2 cups cheese, mixing well.

Spread 1 cup of the sauce in the bottom of a 9 × 13-inch baking dish. Top with one-third of the noodles, then ½ cup sauce. Spoon half the tofu mixture over the noodles and top with another ½ cup sauce. Top with another one-third of the noodles. Press them down firmly into filling. Repeat layers, adding ½ cup sauce, remaining tofu mixture, ½ cup sauce, and remaining noodles. Press noodles down firmly. Spoon remaining sauce over noodles, making sure noodles are totally covered.

Cover and bake 40 minutes. Uncover and continue baking for 20 minutes. Sprinkle remaining 1 cup of mozzarella on top during the last 5 minutes. Let set 10 minutes before cutting into squares and serving.

PER SERVING:
503 Calories; 21g Fat; 24g Protein; 58g Carbohydrate; 9g Dietary Fiber; 34mg Cholesterol; 973mg Sodium. Exchanges: 2 Grain (Starch); 2 Lean Meat; 5½ Vegetable; 3 Fat; 0 Other Carbohydrates.

SERVING SUGGESTIONS: Serve with a big green salad and garlic bread.

ITALIAN CABBAGE SOUP

2 (15.5-ounce) cans cannellini beans, rinsed (or use white beans)

4 tablespoons olive oil

1 medium onion, sliced

½ medium head savoy cabbage, shredded (this is a bit milder, can substitute green cabbage if Savoy is unavailable)

3 garlic cloves, pressed

1 teaspoon dried oregano

5¼ cups low-sodium vegetable broth

Salt and pepper to taste

6 whole wheat country bread slices, cut ½-inch thick (use a loaf of whole wheat bread)

1 cup grated Parmesan or Romano cheese

In a small bowl, mash 1½ cups of beans.

In a soup pot, heat 2 tablespoons oil over medium heat. Add onion and cook, stirring often, till soft, about 3 minutes. Add cabbage, garlic, and oregano; cook, stirring often till cabbage has wilted, about 3 minutes. Add broth, mashed beans, and remaining whole beans; bring to a boil. Reduce heat to medium-low and partially cover, simmering till cabbage is soft, 10 to 12 minutes. Season with salt and pepper.

Shortly before soup is ready, toast bread. Place a slice of bread in each soup bowl. Ladle soup over bread and sprinkle with cheese. Drizzle 1 teaspoon oil over each serving.

PER SERVING:
587 Calories; 18g Fat; 30g Protein; 80g Carbohydrate; 16g Dietary Fiber; 13mg Cholesterol; 1832mg Sodium. Exchanges: 5 Grain (Starch); 2 Lean Meat; ½ Vegetable; 3 Fat.

SERVING SUGGESTIONS: Serve with Carrot Slaw (see page 254) and remaining bread with some butter.

Black and White and Bean All Over

Beans are a staple food in most parts of the world. They are easy to grow, cheap, and highly nutritious. I am of the opinion that everyone, vegetarians and non-vegetarians alike, would do well to include more beans in their diets.

We've talked a little about the benefits of beans, but let's talk particulars. Like cannellini beans, for example. These wonderful big white beans (also called white kidney beans) are tasty in nearly everything. I discovered cannellini beans years ago, and I adore their creamy texture and nutty flavor. I've used cannellini beans in nearly everything from stews, to soups and everything in between, with great results.

Another great bean and more well-known than the cannellini is the black bean, or *frijoles negros,* as they are called. Ever popular and diverse, these black beauties are exceptionally nutritious. It's the black color in their little jackets that impart eight flavonoids not necessarily in your neighboring bean. Flavonoids are the color-producing phytochemicals that give the food its anti-oxidant power. One flavonoid, called anthocyanin, is particularly pronounced in this bean.

Another fantastic attribute of black beans is their omega-3 fatty acids—about three times the amount in other beans. Black beans aren't just wildly popular, they're wildly nutritious, too!

HAWAIIAN SANDWICHES

Serves 6

12 slices whole wheat bread
⅔ cup shredded Cheddar cheese
¾ cup pineapple tidbits in juice, drained
½ cup green bell pepper, seeded, deribbed, and finely chopped
1 cup finely chopped tomatoes

Preheat broiler.

Put six slices of bread on a cookie sheet. Place under broiler and toast slightly. Sprinkle 1½ tablespoons of cheese on each slice.

In a bowl, combine pineapple, green bell pepper, and tomato. Divide evenly among the six cheesy bread slices.

Broil till cheese starts to melt. Top with remaining bread slices and return to broiler. Broil till top slices of bread are toasted.

PER SERVING:
280 Calories; 12g Fat; 13g Protein; 33g Carbohydrate; 5g Dietary Fiber; 30mg Cholesterol; 474mg Sodium. Exchanges: 1½ Grain (Starch); 1 Lean Meat; ½ Vegetable; ½ Fruit; 1½ Fat.

SERVING SUGGESTION: Serve with Clean Out the Fridge Pasta Salad. (Toss together cooked and cooled pasta, chopped veggies—just clean out your crisper—Italian salad dressing, olives, grated cheese, and you're done!)

LENTIL SLOPPY JOES

Serves 6

2 tablespoons olive oil
1 large onion, finely chopped
4 celery stalks, chopped
6 garlic cloves, pressed
¾ teaspoon dried basil
¾ teaspoon dried thyme
Salt and pepper to taste
¾ cup ketchup
⅓ cup water
1½ tablespoons balsamic vinegar
1½ tablespoons brown sugar
1½ tablespoons prepared mustard
3 cups lentils, uncooked
6 whole-grain hamburger buns, toasted

In a skillet, heat oil over medium heat. Add onion and celery and cook, stirring often, till soft, about 5 minutes. Add garlic, basil, thyme, and salt and pepper and cook, stirring, for about 1 minute. Stir in ketchup, water, balsamic vinegar, brown sugar, and mustard. Transfer to slow cooker. Add lentils and mix well.

Cover and cook on low for 4 hours or on high for 2 hours, or till hot and bubbly. Ladle over hot toasted buns.

PER SERVING:
549 Calories; 8g Fat; 32g Protein; 92g Carbohydrate; 32g Dietary Fiber; 0mg Cholesterol; 691mg Sodium. Exchanges: 5 Grain (Starch); 2½ Lean Meat; ½ Vegetable; 0 Fruit; 1½ Fat; ½ Other Carbohydrates.

SERVING SUGGESTIONS: Serve with coleslaw and corn muffins and honey butter.

❀ Week Five

DAY ONE: Penne in Cream Sauce

DAY TWO: Italian Tofu Squares

DAY THREE: Tangy Chickpea Salad

DAY FOUR: Magnificent Mushroom Cheeseburgers

DAY FIVE: Orzo with Spinach and Pine Nuts

DAY SIX: Succulent Sweet Potatoes

SHOPPING LIST

CONDIMENTS

Olive oil

Vegetable oil

Balsamic vinegar

Honey

**Salad dressing (1 meal)

**Caesar dressing (1 meal)

**Mayonnaise (2 meals)

**Rice vinegar (2 meals)

**Toasted sesame oil (1 meal)

**Burger condiments (mayonnaise, mustard, ketchup, relish, etc.; 1 meal)

PRODUCE

1 (14–16-ounce) package firm tofu

3 pounds yellow onions (keep on hand)

2 garlic heads

Mushrooms (1 pound)

1½ pounds green beans

1 head cauliflower

Green leaf lettuce (6 cups)

Baby spinach (3 cups)

3 sweet potatoes

1 bunch basil

1 bunch parsley

**Baby greens (1 meal)

**Romaine lettuce (1 meal)

**Salad toppings (1 meal)

**Coleslaw mix (2 meals)

**Russet potatoes (1 meal)

**Baby carrots (1 meal)

**Tomatoes (1 meal)

**Cilantro (1 meal)

**Burger toppings (onion, lettuce, sliced tomatoes, etc.;
  1 meal)

**1 bunch basil (1 meal)

CANNED GOODS

3 (14.5-ounce) cans low-sodium vegetable broth

3 (14.5-ounce) cans diced tomatoes

2 (15-ounce) cans chickpeas (or use 3 cups dried)

1 (32-ounce) jar spaghetti sauce, your favorite

SPICES AND DRIED HERBS

Oregano

Rosemary

Cumin

Garlic powder

Onion flakes

DAIRY/DAIRY CASE

Butter

Eggs (6)

Egg whites (6)

Skim milk

Light sour cream (¾ cup)

Low-fat cottage cheese (1½ cups)

Cheddar cheese (6 slices)

Grated Parmesan cheese (1½ cups); **additional ½ cup

**Sliced mozzarella cheese (1 meal)

DRY GOODS

All-purpose flour

Whole wheat flour

Baking powder

Wheat germ (½ cup)

Penne pasta (12 ounces)

Orzo (2 cups)

Pearl barley (2¼ cups)

Chickpeas (3 cups dried if not using canned)

Bread crumbs

Pine nuts (⅓ cup)

**Dry-roasted peanuts (1 meal)

**Croutons (packaged)

BREADS/BAKERY

6 whole wheat hamburger buns

**Garlic Bread (1 meal)

**Whole-grain rolls (1 meal)

**Corn muffins (1 meal) or make your own

PENNE IN CREAM SAUCE

Serves 6

"This was my favorite—I've cooked vegetables at the end of cooking pasta for several years but not beans. I think the bean and basil combination was really good."   —Jan B.

    12 ounces penne pasta
    1½ pounds green beans, sliced in half
    1½ cups cauliflower florets
    3 tablespoons olive oil
    1 large onion, chopped
    3 garlic cloves, pressed
    3 (14.5-ounce) cans diced tomatoes, drained
    ¾ cup light sour cream
    3 tablespoons skim milk
    ½ cup grated Parmesan cheese
    3 tablespoons chopped fresh basil

Cook pasta according to package directions until al dente, adding green beans and cauliflower in the last 3 minutes of cooking. Drain well and return to pot.

In a large skillet, heat oil over medium heat. Add onion and garlic and cook, stirring often, till soft, about 3 minutes. Add tomatoes and cook about 4 minutes, till hot.

Remove skillet from heat and stir in sour cream, skim milk, Parmesan cheese, and basil till combined. Pour cream sauce over penne and toss thoroughly to coat.

PER SERVING:
428 Calories; 16g Fat; 14g Protein; 58g Carbohydrate; 7g Dietary Fiber; 18mg Cholesterol; 167mg Sodium. Exchanges: 2½ Grain (Starch); ½ Lean Meat; 2½ Vegetable; 0 Non-Fat Milk; 2½ Fat.

SERVING SUGGESTIONS: Serve with a simple green salad (I like baby greens with this rich dish) and garlic bread.

ITALIAN TOFU SQUARES

1 (14–16-ounce) package firm tofu, sliced, drained well
6 eggs
1½ cups low-fat cottage cheese
¼ cup grated Parmesan cheese
3 tablespoons onion flakes
1½ tablespoons all-purpose flour
1½ teaspoons dried oregano
Salt and pepper to taste
½ tablespoon garlic powder
1½ tablespoons chopped fresh parsley
4½ tablespoons dry bread crumbs
3 tablespoons butter
1 (32-ounce) jar spaghetti sauce

Preheat oven to 350 degrees F. Grease a 9-inch square baking dish. Slice tofu and drain well between paper towels.

In a blender, combine tofu, eggs, cottage cheese, 1½ tablespoons of the Parmesan cheese, onion flakes, flour, oregano, salt and pepper, garlic powder, and parsley. Blend till smooth. Pour mixture into baking dish.

In a small bowl, combine bread crumbs with remaining Parmesan cheese and sprinkle evenly over top of tofu mixture. Dot with butter.

Bake 35 minutes, till set and lightly browned. Cut into squares to serve.

Meanwhile, in a saucepan, heat spaghetti sauce. Pour over tofu squares.

PER SERVING:
429 Calories; 23g Fat; 23g Protein; 35g Carbohydrate; 6g Dietary Fiber; 237mg Cholesterol; 1330mg Sodium. Exchanges: ½ Grain (Starch); 2½ Lean Meat; 4½ Vegetable; 3½ Fat.

SERVING SUGGESTIONS: Serve with a Caesar Salad (see page 256) and whole-grain rolls.

TANGY CHICKPEA SALAD

Serves 6

3 cups cooked chickpeas (or equivalent canned; drain and rinse)
1 small onion, finely chopped
4 tablespoons balsamic vinegar
2 tablespoons olive oil
3 tablespoons water
¼ teaspoon garlic powder
1 teaspoon honey
Salt and pepper to taste
6 cups green leaf lettuce, torn into bite-size pieces

In a bowl, combine chickpeas and onion. Mix well.

In a small bowl, combine remaining ingredients except lettuce. Add to beans, mixing well.

Chill several hours, stirring every once in a while. Serve over a bed of lettuce.

PER SERVING:
422 Calories; 11g Fat; 20g Protein; 65g Carbohydrate; 18g Dietary Fiber; 0mg Cholesterol; 30mg Sodium. Exchanges: 4 Grain (Starch); 1 Lean Meat; ½ Vegetable; 0 Fruit; 1½ Fat; 0 Other Carbohydrates.

SERVING SUGGESTION: Serve with corn muffins.

MAGNIFICENT MUSHROOM CHEESEBURGERS

Serves 6

"A very tasty alternative to garden burgers."   —Angela C.

½ cup plus 1 tablespoon whole wheat flour
½ cup plus 1 tablespoon wheat germ
¾ teaspoon baking powder
Salt and pepper to taste
⅛ teaspoon dried oregano
¼ teaspoon cumin
¼ teaspoon garlic powder
6 egg whites
1 small onion, finely chopped
3 cups mushrooms, cleaned and chopped
1 tablespoon vegetable oil
6 slices Cheddar cheese
6 whole wheat hamburger buns

In a medium bowl, combine flour, wheat germ, baking powder, and spices. Mix well.

In another bowl, combine egg whites, onion, and mushrooms. Add to dry mixture, mixing till all ingredients are moistened. Shape into six patties, wetting hands if necessary, to prevent sticking.

In a skillet, heat oil over medium heat. Add patties and cook till nicely browned on each side. Top with cheese and heat till cheese is melted. Serve on hamburger buns.

PER SERVING:
364 Calories; 15g Fat; 19g Protein; 39g Carbohydrate; 5g Dietary Fiber; 30mg Cholesterol; 536mg Sodium. Exchanges: 2½ Grain (Starch); 1½ Lean Meat; ½ Vegetable; 2 Fat; 0 Other Carbohydrates.

SERVING SUGGESTIONS: Serve with coleslaw, Oven Fries (see page 257), and condiments for your burger—mayo, mustard, ketchup, relish, onion, lettuce, and sliced tomato.

ORZO WITH SPINACH AND PINE NUTS

Serves 6

6 tablespoons pine nuts
3 tablespoons butter, melted
1 large onion, chopped
3 garlic cloves, pressed
4½ cups water
2 cups orzo
Salt and pepper to taste
3 cups chopped baby spinach, tightly packed
¾ cup grated Parmesan cheese

In a small skillet, spread pine nuts and cook, stirring often, over medium heat for 2 minutes. Set aside.

In a saucepan, heat butter over medium heat. Add onion and garlic, and sauté for 5 minutes. Add water, orzo, and salt and pepper; bring to a boil. Reduce heat and cook about 10 minutes, till liquid is absorbed. Stir in spinach, cheese, and toasted pine nuts.

PER SERVING:
365 Calories; 14g Fat; 14g Protein; 46g Carbohydrate; 2g Dietary Fiber; 23mg Cholesterol; 266mg Sodium. Exchanges: 3 Grain (Starch); 1 Lean Meat; ½ Vegetable; 2½ Fat.

SERVING SUGGESTION: Serve with Caprese Salad (alternate layers of sliced tomato, sliced mozzarella, and basil leaves; drizzle with olive oil and serve with freshly ground pepper).

SUCCULENT SWEET POTATOES

Serves 6

2 tablespoons olive oil
2 large onions, finely chopped
3 garlic cloves, pressed
¾ teaspoon dried rosemary
2¼ cups pearl barley, rinsed
4½ cups low-sodium vegetable stock
3 sweet potatoes, peeled and cut into ¼-inch cubes

In a skillet, heat oil over medium heat. Add onion and sauté till soft, about 3 to 4 minutes. Add garlic and rosemary, and cook, stirring, for 1 minute. Stir in barley till well coated. Add broth and bring to a boil.

Place sweet potatoes in slow cooker. Pour barley mixture over sweet potatoes and mix well. Cover and cook on low for 8 hours or on high for 4 hours, till barley and sweet potatoes are tender.

PER SERVING:
510 Calories; 9g Fat; 13g Protein; 98g Carbohydrate; 17g Dietary Fiber; 2mg Cholesterol; 1236mg Sodium. Exchanges: 6 Grain (Starch); ½ Vegetable; 1½ Fat.

SERVING SUGGESTIONS: Serve potatoes with Asian Coleslaw (see page 254) and a bowl of baby carrots.

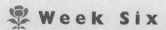 # Week Six

DAY ONE: Macaroni Salad

DAY TWO: Broccoli Tofu Patties

DAY THREE: Mock Tuna Salad

DAY FOUR: Confetti Salad

DAY FIVE: Oat Burgers Parmigiana

DAY SIX: Tortilla Soup

SHOPPING LIST

CONDIMENTS

Olive oil

Vegetable oil

Balsamic vinegar

Dijon mustard

Mayonnaise

Sweet pickle relish

**Honey (1 meal)

**Salad dressing (3 meals)

**Rice vinegar (2 meals)

**BBQ sauce, your favorite (1 meal)

**Burger condiments (mayonnaise, mustard, ketchup,
   relish, etc.; 1 meal)

PRODUCE

1 (14–16-ounce) package firm tofu

3 pounds yellow onions (keep on hand);
   **additional (1 meal)

1 red onion

2 bunches green onions

1 garlic head

1 red bell pepper

1 dried green chili

1 bunch celery

5 carrots; **additional (1 meal)

1 bunch broccoli; **additional (1 meal)

1 head cauliflower

Green leaf lettuce (6 cups)

2 avocados

1 lime

1 bunch cilantro

**Tomatoes (1 meal)

**Grape tomatoes (1 meal)

**Spinach (2 meals)

**Coleslaw mix (1 meal)

**Lettuce, not iceberg (1 meal)

**Salad toppings (3 meals)

**Baby carrots (2 meals)

**Burger toppings (onion, lettuce, sliced tomatoes, etc.;
   1 meal)

CANNED GOODS

4 (14.5-ounce) cans low-sodium vegetable broth

1 (28-ounce) can diced tomatoes

2 (16-ounce) cans great northern beans

1 (16-ounce) can pinto beans

1 (4.5-ounce) can green chili peppers

1 (28-ounce) jar spaghetti sauce, your favorite

SPICES AND DRIED HERBS

Italian seasoning

Oregano

Rosemary

Red pepper flakes

Garlic powder

Cumin

Chili powder

DAIRY/DAIRY CASE

Eggs (5)

Sour cream (1 cup)

Shredded Cheddar cheese (1½ cups);
   **additional (1 meal)

Shredded mozzarella cheese (1 cup)

Grated Parmesan cheese (optional garnish);
   **additional (1 meal)

**Shredded cheese, your choice (Cheddar/Jack
   blend recommended) (1 meal)

**Butter (1 meal)

DRY GOODS

All-purpose flour

Whole wheat flour

Sugar

Baking powder

Wheat germ

Elbow macaroni (1 pound)

Rolled oats (2 cups)

**Raisins (1 meal)

**Walnuts (1 meal)

**Fettuccine noodles (1 meal)

BREADS/BAKERY

6 whole wheat bagels

3 corn tortillas

**Whole wheat tortillas (1 meal)

**Whole-grain bread (1 meal)

**Corn muffins (1 meal)

FROZEN FOODS

1 (16-ounce) package whole kernel corn

1 (10-ounce) package frozen green beans

MACARONI SALAD

Serves 6

1 (10-ounce) package frozen green beans, cooked
1 pound elbow macaroni, cooked
1 cup shredded carrots
1 cup sliced celery
¼ cup chopped green onions
1½ cups shredded Cheddar cheese
½ cup Italian salad dressing
¼ teaspoon dried oregano

In a large bowl, combine green beans, macaroni, carrots, celery, green onions, and cheese. Toss till blended. Add remaining ingredients and mix well.

Chill to blend flavors, stirring occasionally.

PER SERVING:
430 Calories; 20g Fat; 15g Protein; 48g Carbohydrate; 4g Dietary Fiber; 30mg Cholesterol; 361mg Sodium. Exchanges: 2½ Grain (Starch); 1 Lean Meat; 1½ Vegetable; 0 Fruit; 3 Fat.

SERVING SUGGESTIONS: Serve with grilled tomato cheese sandwiches (made with whole-grain bread, sliced tomatoes, and sliced Cheddar cheese—easy!) and a spinach salad.

BROCCOLI TOFU PATTIES

Serves 6

1 (14–16-ounce) package firm tofu, drained and sliced

3 eggs

¾ teaspoon dried rosemary

½ teaspoon red pepper flakes

1 large onion, chopped

1½ tablespoons all-purpose flour

1½ teaspoons baking powder

1½ cups cooked and chopped broccoli

1 tablespoon vegetable oil

Slice tofu and drain well between paper towels.

In a large bowl, combine tofu with remaining ingredients except broccoli and oil. Mash with a fork till well blended.

Stir in broccoli. Form mixture into six patties.

In a large skillet, heat oil over medium heat and add patties. Cook on both sides till browned, about 5 minutes.

PER SERVING:
135 Calories; 8g Fat; 10g Protein; 7g Carbohydrate; 1g Dietary Fiber; 106mg Cholesterol; 168mg Sodium. Exchanges: ½ Grain (Starch); 2 Lean Meat; ½ Vegetable; 1 Fat; 0 Other Carbohydrates.

SERVING SUGGESTIONS: Serve with Carrot Slaw (see page 254), Oven Fries (see page 257), and condiments for your burger—mayo, mustard, ketchup, relish, onion, lettuce and sliced tomato.

MOCK TUNA SALAD

Serves 6

2 (16-ounce) cans great northern beans, rinsed and drained

3 tablespoons chopped onion

3 tablespoons sweet pickle relish

¼ cup chopped celery

2 tablespoons mayonnaise (or more, depending on the texture and
   moistness you like)

2 hard-boiled eggs, chopped

Dash of garlic powder

Salt and pepper to taste

6 whole wheat bagels, split and toasted

Place beans in a bowl and mash with a fork. Add remaining ingredients except bagels and mix well. Serve open faced on toasted bagels.

PER SERVING:
445 Calories; 7g Fat; 20g Protein; 75g Carbohydrate; 8g Dietary Fiber; 72mg Cholesterol; 600mg Sodium. Exchanges: 4½ Grain (Starch); 1 Lean Meat; 0 Vegetable; ½ Fat.

SERVING SUGGESTIONS: Serve with coleslaw and baby carrots.

DO AHEAD TIP: Tomorrow night's salad tastes better if allowed to chill overnight. Since dinner was so easy tonight, go ahead and throw together the salad for tomorrow night and get it chillin'.

CONFETTI SALAD

Serves 6

1½ cups cauliflower florets
¾ cup shredded carrots
¾ cup cored, seeded, and chopped red bell pepper
1½ tablespoons olive oil
1½ tablespoons balsamic vinegar
1½ tablespoons water
1½ teaspoons Dijon mustard
1½ teaspoons sugar
⅛ teaspoon garlic powder
3 tablespoons green onions, chopped, whites and part of green tops
6 cups green leaf lettuce, torn into bite-size pieces

In a medium bowl, combine cauliflower, carrots, and red bell pepper.

In a small bowl, combine remaining ingredients except green onions and lettuce. Add to veggies, mixing well.

Chill overnight. Serve on a bed of lettuce and garnish with green onions.

PER SERVING:
61 Calories; 4g Fat; 2g Protein; 7g Carbohydrate; 2g Dietary Fiber; 0mg Cholesterol; 34mg Sodium. Exchanges: 0 Grain (Starch); 0 Lean Meat; 1 Vegetable; 0 Fruit; ½ Fat; 0 Other Carbohydrates.

SERVING SUGGESTIONS: Serve with BBQ Quesadillas (see page 258). Add a bowl of baby carrots and one of grape tomatoes.

OAT BURGERS PARMIGIANA

Serves 6

2 tablespoons vegetable oil
1 large onion, finely chopped
2 garlic cloves, pressed
2 cups rolled oats
½ cup wheat germ
½ cup whole wheat flour
2 teaspoons Italian seasoning
Salt and pepper to taste
1⅔ cups water
1 (28-ounce) jar spaghetti sauce
1 cup shredded mozzarella cheese
Grated Parmesan cheese for garnish

Preheat oven to 350 degrees F. Lightly grease a cookie sheet.

In a skillet, heat oil over medium heat. Add onion and garlic; sauté till onion starts to brown, about 10 minutes.

In a large bowl, combine oats, wheat germ, flour, and spices. Mix well. Add water and cooked onion and garlic. Mix well till combined.

Form six patties and place on cookie sheet. Bake for 25 minutes.

Meanwhile, in a saucepan, heat spaghetti sauce.

Divide mozzarella evenly among patties and bake for 5 minutes. Top each patty with ½ cup hot spaghetti sauce. Sprinkle with Parmesan cheese, if you like.

PER SERVING:
464 Calories; 21g Fat; 17g Protein; 56g Carbohydrate; 11g Dietary Fiber; 25mg Cholesterol; 780mg Sodium. Exchanges: 2 Grain (Starch); 1 Lean Meat; 5 Vegetable; 3½ Fat.

SERVING SUGGESTIONS: Serve with hot cooked fettuccine noodles sprinkled with Parmesan cheese. Add steamed broccoli and a big green salad.

The Zest Is Yet to Come

Adding zest to a dish gives it that extra "something" that sets it apart from similar dishes.

Zest is, if you are wondering, the colorful peel on citrus fruit—the orange on an orange, green on a lime, yellow on a lemon, and so on. But just the colored part of the rind—the white pith underneath the skin is bitter. To use the zest (and you get it by using either a zester, made specifically for this job, a vegetable peeler, or a knife), you will then want to chop it further, as you want to make sure it's in teeny tiny bits or it will completely overwhelm the dish.

It's the zing in the zest that does the trick!

TORTILLA SOUP

Serves 6

"My husband took a few bites and said, 'Wow, this is really good!' We are Texans and love Tex-Mex food. I love that it's for the slow cooker and easy as well as good."   —Lisa S.

1 dried green chili pepper
2 cups boiling water
1 tablespoon olive oil
2 onions, chopped
2 garlic cloves, pressed
2 teaspoons cumin
1 tablespoon chili powder
1 teaspoon lime zest (see sidebar)
Salt and pepper to taste
1 (16-ounce) can pinto beans, rinsed and drained
1 (28-ounce) can diced tomatoes, drained with juice reserved
6 cups low-sodium vegetable broth
1 (4.5-ounce) can mild green chili peppers, drained and chopped
2 cups frozen corn, thawed
¼ cup vegetable oil (for brushing the tortilla strips)
3 corn tortillas, cut into ½-inch strips
2 avocados, cut into ½-inch cubes
1 cup finely chopped red onion
1 cup sour cream
1 bunch finely chopped cilantro

In a heatproof bowl, soak chili pepper in boiling water for 30 minutes. Drain and discard stems and water. Set aside.

In a skillet, heat olive oil over medium heat. Add onions and cook till soft, about 5 minutes. Add garlic, cumin, chili powder, lime zest, salt and pepper, and reserved chili and cook for an additional minute. Transfer mixture to food processor along with beans and 1 cup tomato liquid and process till smooth.

Transfer processed mixture to a slow cooker. Add tomatoes and broth, mixing well. Cover and cook on low for 8 to 10 hours or on high for 3 to 4 hours. Stir in mild green chilies and corn. Cover and cook on high for another 15 to 20 minutes.

Meanwhile, preheat oven to 400 degrees F. Brush tortilla strips with oil, place on cookie sheet, and bake for 4 minutes on each side, till crisp.

To serve, ladle soup into bowls and top with tortilla strips, avocado, red onion, sour cream, and cilantro.

PER SERVING:
630 Calories; 40g Fat; 23g Protein; 53g Carbohydrate; 13g Dietary Fiber; 17mg Cholesterol; 1158mg Sodium. Exchanges: 2 Grain (Starch); 1½ Lean Meat; 2½ Vegetable; ½ Fruit; 0 Non-Fat Milk; 8 Fat.

SERVING SUGGESTIONS: Serve with a big spinach salad, corn muffins, and honey butter.

SUMMER

☀ Week One

DAY ONE: Chinese Tofu and Eggplant Stir-Fry

DAY TWO: Kaleidoscope Rotini

DAY THREE: Minty Lentils

DAY FOUR: Sunny Summer Salad

DAY FIVE: Grilled Portobello Mushrooms

DAY SIX: Tempeh-Stuffed Peppers

SHOPPING LIST

CONDIMENTS

Olive oil

Vegetable oil

Vinegar (if using white grape juice)

Apple cider vinegar

Balsamic vinegar

Red wine vinegar

White wine (instead of saki or white grape juice)

White grape juice (instead of saki or white wine)

Saki (or white wine or white grape juice)

Dijon mustard

Soy sauce, low-sodium if available

Kalamata olives (½ cup)

**Mayonnaise (2 meals)

**Horseradish (1 meal)

**Salad dressing, your choice (3 meals)

**Burger condiments (ketchup, mayo, mustard, relish, etc.;
   1 meal)

**Rice vinegar (1 meal)

PRODUCE

1 (14–16-ounce) package firm tofu

1 (6-ounce) package tempeh (near the tofu in produce section)

3 pounds yellow onions (keep on hand)

1 large red onion

2–3 bunches green onions

2 garlic heads

7 large green bell peppers

6 large portobello mushrooms

1 large carrot

4 large tomatoes

10 roma tomatoes

2 large eggplants

2 lemons (for 4 tablespoons juice)

4 tangerines

1 bunch cilantro

1 bunch parsley

1 bunch thyme

1 bunch basil

1 bunch mint

**Lettuce, not iceberg (2 meals)

**Spinach (1 meal)

**Salad toppings (3 meals)

**Baby carrots (2 meals)

**Grape tomatoes (1 meal)

**Celery (1 meal)

**Broccoli florets (1 meal)

**Cauliflower florets (1 meal)

**Coleslaw mix (1 meal)

**Yellow summer squash (1 meal)

**Zucchini (1 meal)

CANNED GOODS

3 (14.5-ounce) cans crushed tomatoes

1 (15-ounce) can chickpeas (also called garbanzo beans)

SPICES AND DRIED HERBS

Ground ginger

Cayenne pepper

DAIRY/DAIRY CASE

Butter

Crumbled feta cheese (1 cup)

Shredded Cheddar cheese (2½ cups)

**Sour cream

DRY GOODS

Cornstarch

Brown sugar

Rotini pasta (12 ounces)

Farfalle or bowtie pasta (1¼ cups)

Brown rice (5⅛ cups)

Green lentils (2½ cups)

Walnut pieces (⅓ cup)

BREADS/BAKERY

**Garlic bread (1 meal)

**Whole wheat hamburger buns (1 meal)

CHINESE TOFU AND EGGPLANT STIR-FRY

Serves 6

4½ tablespoons low-sodium soy sauce

¾ cup saki, or white wine or grape juice with a splash of vinegar

1½ tablespoons brown sugar

1½ tablespoons apple cider vinegar

2½ tablespoons cornstarch

3 tablespoons vegetable oil

1 large onion, thinly sliced

2 medium–large eggplants, cut into strips (first cut thin lengthwise slices and then cut across)

6 garlic cloves, pressed

2 teaspoons ground ginger

Salt and pepper to taste

Pinch of cayenne pepper (more or less depending on your heat tolerance)

1 (14–16-ounce) package firm tofu, drained, pressed, and cut into strips

12 green onions, green part chopped and white parts cut into strips

6 cups cooked brown rice

1 bunch chopped cilantro, (stems and leaves)

In a mixing bowl, combine soy sauce, saki, brown sugar, and vinegar. Stir to dissolve brown sugar. Next add cornstarch and whisk until dissolved. Set aside.

In a large skillet, heat oil over medium-high heat and sauté onion for about 1 minute.

Add eggplant and cook until soft, 8 to 10 minutes. Add garlic, ginger, salt and pepper, and cayenne and cook a few more minutes.

Last, add tofu and white part of the green onions to skillet.

Give the soy sauce mixture a quick stir and add to skillet. Mix well and cook another few minutes, until the sauce thickens.

Remove from heat and serve over brown rice, topped with green part of chopped green onions and fresh cilantro.

PER SERVING:
416 Calories; 10g Fat; 9g Protein; 67g Carbohydrate; 8g Dietary Fiber; 0mg Cholesterol; 465mg Sodium. Exchanges: 3 Grain (Starch); ½ Lean Meat; 2½ Vegetable; 0 Fruit; 1½ Fat; 0 Other Carbohydrates.

SERVING SUGGESTION: Serve with a big green salad.

DO AHEAD TIP: Prepare rotini for next night and chill overnight so chilling the prepared salad won't be necessary.

KALEIDOSCOPE ROTINI

12 ounces rotini pasta

3 cups seeded and diced tomatoes

½ cup seeded, deribbed, and finely diced green bell pepper

2 green onions, thinly sliced (white parts only)

1 garlic clove, pressed

¼ cup olive oil

1 cup crumbled feta cheese

½ cup Kalamata olives, pitted and coarsely chopped

2 tablespoons chopped fresh parsley

2 tablespoons chopped fresh thyme

2 tablespoons balsamic vinegar

1 tablespoon red wine vinegar

1 tablespoon lemon juice

Salt and pepper to taste

Prepare pasta according to package directions until al dente. Drain and set aside.

While pasta is cooking, in a large bowl combine tomatoes, bell pepper, green onions, garlic, and olive oil; toss to mix well. Add feta cheese, olives, parsley, thyme, balsamic vinegar, red wine vinegar, and lemon juice; toss again.

Toss pasta with veggie mixture, season with salt and pepper, and serve.

Chill before serving, if desired.

PER SERVING:
436 Calories; 21g Fat; 12g Protein; 51g Carbohydrate; 3g Dietary Fiber; 22mg Cholesterol; 607mg Sodium. Exchanges: 3 Grain (Starch); ½ Lean Meat; 1 Vegetable; 0 Fruit; 3½ Fat; 0 Other Carbohydrates

SERVING SUGGESTIONS: Garlic bread and a big spinach salad ought to do the trick.

DO AHEAD TIP: Prepare lentils and rice for tomorrow night's meal.

Waves of Grain

Most vegetarians, thankfully, understand the goodness of eating whole grains (as opposed to the refined versions). Whole oats, barley, and more obscure grains like quinoa, millet, amaranth, and kamut are all better when left whole and not messed with. Making them is a snap—follow the directions on the package! That won't work if you buy from the bulk bins, but considering the questionable cleanliness of some of those bulk bins, I'd steer way clear and opt for the slightly more expensive, more hygienically sound packaged food. I once saw a little boy about 3 years old having himself a little buffet experience meandering through those bins. I can't imagine the bins are cleaned and sanitized too often, either.

Once you've purchased your grains of choice, it's quite simple to keep them in little containers in your fridge to serve as the basis of a quick meal—just add beans, or tempeh, or some leftover veggies; zap in the microwave; and you have yourself a quick little lunch.

MINTY LENTILS

Serves 6

"Delicious!!! Such a surprise to get a lovely bowl of comfort food from very simple ingredients—love it!" —Annabel in Australia

1¼ cups farfalle or bowtie pasta
2 tablespoons olive oil
1 large red onion, chopped
10 roma tomatoes, seeded and diced
Salt and pepper to taste
2½ cups green lentils, cooked
2 cups cooked brown rice
½ cup water
7 tablespoons butter
3½ tablespoons chopped fresh mint leaves

Cook pasta according to package directions until al dente. Drain and set aside.

In a skillet, heat oil over medium-high heat and sauté onion, stirring occasionally, until well browned, 12 to 15 minutes. Add tomatoes and season with salt and pepper; remove onion and tomatoes from skillet to a serving platter and set aside.

In the same skillet, heat lentils, rice, and pasta with ½ cup water. Season with salt and pepper and return tomatoes and onion to pan. Turn heat down to low and allow all ingredients to simmer and warm through.

In a small saucepan, heat butter over medium-high heat. Add mint leaves and cook for 30 seconds. Grind in fresh pepper. Pour the mint butter over the lentil mixture and serve.

PER SERVING:
473 Calories; 21g Fat; 14g Protein; 60g Carbohydrate; 11g Dietary Fiber; 36mg Cholesterol; 161mg Sodium. Exchanges: 3 Grain (Starch); ½ Lean Meat; 2½ Vegetable; 4 Fat.

SERVING SUGGESTIONS: Serve with a big green salad and a bowl of baby carrots for the table.

DO AHEAD TIP: Make the Sunny Summer Salad and refrigerate overnight.

Serves 6

4 tangerines

3 tablespoons lemon juice

¼ cup olive oil

¼ teaspoon Dijon mustard

Salt and pepper to taste

1 tablespoon fresh thyme

1½ cups canned chickpeas, rinsed and drained

3 green onions, sliced

1 large carrot, shredded

⅓ cup walnut pieces, toasted

Zest one of the tangerines into a mixing bowl. Be careful to only use the orange part of the peel, as the white part (the pith) is bitter.

Into same mixing bowl, squeeze in all the juice from zested tangerine. Whisk in lemon juice and then slowly add oil. When oil is mixed in, whisk in mustard, salt and pepper, and thyme.

Section remaining tangerines and add them along with chickpeas, green onions, carrot, and walnuts; toss to coat. Chill salad for about 30 minutes before serving, if desired.

PER SERVING:
228 Calories; 14g Fat; 5g Protein; 23g Carbohydrate; 5g Dietary Fiber; 0mg Cholesterol; 188mg Sodium. Exchanges: 1 Grain (Starch); 0 Lean Meat; ½ Vegetable; ½ Fruit; 2½ Fat; 0 Other Carbohydrates.

SERVING SUGGESTIONS: Serve with a nice big relish plate of grape tomatoes, baby carrots, cut-up celery, broccoli and cauliflower florets, and an easy dip made with half sour cream and half mayo, and horseradish to taste.

A Fungus Among Us

The once gourmet, elusive portobello mushroom has become commonplace in grocery stores. An excellent source of niacin, potassium, and selenium, portobellos are delicious grilled and eaten as a main course on buns or sliced and stirred into stir-fries. The taste of portobellos has been described as meaty, although I'm loath to call it that in a book such as this.

Preparing portobellos is simple. Wash carefully in cool water and dry with a paper towel, but only just before preparing, otherwise portobellos should be stored in brown paper bags in the fridge for optimum freshness. They should last a week to 10 days when stored this way.

Portobellos, like most mushrooms, have "gills" on the underside of their enormous caps. Those black gills can get nasty when you're cooking and they'll put black spores on everything they touch. To alleviate this problem, eliminate the gills—take a small spoon and scoop 'em out. It's easy to do and it will make your portobellos picture-perfect!

GRILLED PORTOBELLO MUSHROOMS

Serves 6

3 garlic cloves, pressed
3 teaspoons chopped fresh basil
Salt and pepper to taste
3 tablespoons balsamic vinegar
½ cup olive oil
6 large portobello mushrooms, stems removed

Preheat outdoor grill, indoor grill, or broiler.

In a small bowl, combine garlic, basil, salt and pepper, vinegar, and oil. Whisk until blended.

Brush both sides of mushrooms with oil mixture. Salt and pepper to taste.

On a medium-hot grill, cook mushrooms until tender and slightly browned, turning once (8–10 minutes). Serve whole or sliced into strips.

PER SERVING:
202 Calories; 19g Fat; 3g Protein; 8g Carbohydrate; 2g Dietary Fiber; 0mg Cholesterol; 7mg Sodium. Exchanges: 1½ Vegetable; 0 Fruit; 3½ Fat.

SERVING SUGGESTIONS: Serve grilled mushrooms on buns with all the condiments like a hamburger. Add a side of coleslaw (coleslaw mix, mayonnaise, and rice vinegar) and you're there!

DO AHEAD TIP: Cook rice for tomorrow night's meal.

Tempeh Tantrum

Tempeh can be a little temperamental, so you need a little "tempeh knowledge" for how to handle it.

1. Tempeh absorbs the flavors of what it is cooked with, which makes it a great filler for things like the Tempeh-Stuffed Peppers (page 138).
2. Tempeh absorbs liquid. The earlier you add the liquid, the more it will absorb. If you have added too much liquid, tempeh can come to the rescue. But if you don't watch what you are doing, it'll be dry.

TEMPEH-STUFFED PEPPERS

Serves 6

6 ounces tempeh, cubed
½ cup water (or more if needed)
1 large garlic clove, pressed
3 (14.5-ounce) cans crushed tomatoes
1 large onion, chopped
2¼ cups cooked brown rice
2½ cups shredded Cheddar cheese
6 green bell peepers, tops cut off and seeded

In a saucepan, steam tempeh with a little water, about ½ cup, for about 5 minutes on medium-low heat. Let tempeh cool for a minute. In a bowl, mash steamed tempeh with garlic and half the tomatoes.

Stir in onion, rice, and 1½ cups cheese. Stuff peppers with mixture.

Place peppers in slow cooker. Pour remaining half of the tomatoes over peppers. Cover. Cook on low 6 to 8 hours or on high 3 to 4 hours. Top with remaining cheese during last 30 minutes.

PER SERVING:
390 Calories; 5g Fat; 14g Protein; 77g Carbohydrate; 6g Dietary Fiber; 0mg Cholesterol; 301mg Sodium. Exchanges: 4 Grain (Starch); ½ Lean Meat; 3 Vegetable; ½ Fat.

SERVING SUGGESTIONS: Serve with sautéed yellow summer squash and zucchini.

✳ Week Two

DAY ONE: Rigatoni and Broccoli Salad

DAY TWO: Crusty Tofu

DAY THREE: Southwestern Black Beans

DAY FOUR: Raspberry Salad

DAY FIVE: Grilled Vegetable Quesadillas

DAY SIX: Another Nutty Lentil Loaf

SHOPPING LIST

CONDIMENTS

Olive oil

Vegetable oil

Red wine vinegar

Dijon mustard

Honey

Salad dressing, your choice; **additional (2 meals)

**Horseradish (1 meal)

**Mayonnaise (1 meal)

**Salsa, your favorite (1 meal)

PRODUCE

1 (14–16-ounce) package extra-firm tofu

3 pounds yellow onions (keep on hand)

1 head garlic; **additional

2 red bell peppers

1 bunch celery; **additional (1 meal)

1 cup mushrooms

Carrots (enough for 2 cups shredded)

2 bunches broccoli; **additional (1 meal)

4 large tomatoes; **additional (1 meal)

1 English cucumber

1 medium zucchini; **additional (1 meal)

1 medium yellow summer squash

3 ears corn on the cob, (if not using frozen);
   **additional (1 meal)

1 head romaine lettuce

1 head red cabbage

2 lemons (for 2 tablespoons juice)

1 bunch cilantro; **additional

1 bunch chives

1 bunch basil

1 bunch parsley

2 cups raspberries

**Grape tomatoes (1 meal)

**Baby carrots (1 meal)

**Cauliflower (1 meal)

**Lettuce, not iceberg (2 meals)

**Salad toppings (2 meals)

CANNED GOODS

1 (28-ounce) can black beans

Chipotle chilies in adobo

SPICES AND DRIED HERBS

Basil

Paprika

Chili powder

Cumin

DAIRY/DAIRY CASE

Eggs (3)

Cheddar cheese (¾ cup cubed, 3 cups shredded)

Shredded low-fat Monterey Jack cheese (2 cups)

**Shredded Cheddar/Jack blend (1 meal)

**Sour cream (2 meals)

**Sliced cheese, your favorite (1 meal)

DRY GOODS

Rigatoni pasta (4½ cups)

Brown lentils (2 cups)

Pine nuts (⅔ cup)

Cashews (1 cup)

Dried cranberries (¼ cup)

Seasoned bread crumbs

**Brown rice (1 meal)

BREADS/BAKERY

12 whole wheat tortillas

**Croissants (1 meal)

FROZEN FOODS

1 (32-ounce) bag frozen corn kernels (if not using fresh
corn)

RIGATONI AND BROCCOLI SALAD

Serves 6

2 bunches broccoli, cut into florets, stalks diced
4½ cups rigatoni pasta
1 cup diced tomato
½ cup pine nuts
¾ cup cubed Cheddar cheese
1½ tablespoons chopped fresh basil
1 cup salad dressing
Salt and pepper to taste

Bring a large stockpot filled with water to a boil. Add broccoli and blanch for about 2 minutes. Remove and place in a bowl. Rinse under cold water until chilled. Drain completely and pat dry with paper towels. Place in a large serving bowl.

Cook rigatoni in the boiling water according to package directions until al dente. Drain in a colander, rinsing with cold water until chilled. Drain again and pat with paper towels to get rid of moisture. Place in bowl with broccoli.

Stir in tomato, pine nuts, cheese, and basil. Pour your favorite dressing on the salad. Season with salt and pepper. Chill before serving or serve as is.

PER SERVING:
486 Calories; 31g Fat; 16g Protein; 42g Carbohydrate; 6g Dietary Fiber; 15mg Cholesterol; 440mg Sodium. Exchanges: 2 Grain (Starch); 1 Lean Meat; 1½ Vegetable; ½ Fruit; 5½ Fat.

SERVING SUGGESTIONS: Serve with a big relish plate of grape tomatoes, baby carrots, cut-up celery, cauliflower florets, and an easy dip made with half sour cream and half mayo, and horseradish to taste.

The Protein Bar

Belly up and let's take a look at how to boost your protein intake with the following foods:

- *Tempeh.* Great in stir-fries and the king of protein, weighing in at 41g per 1 cup.
- *Veggie patties.* Makes a great sandwich with nearly no preparation, 31g per patty.
- *Seitan.* Pronounced *say-tan,* it is extracted wheat gluten made into a mock meat product. Seitan is a heavy-duty protein source, and packaged seitan can be a good substitute for tempeh in stir-fries. Seitan contains a hefty 31g protein per 3 ounces.
- *Tofu.* No slouch in the protein department, 4 ounces of tofu equals 11g of protein.
- *Legumes and beans.* Beans and legumes vary slightly in protein content, with 1 cup of lentils measuring 18g, black beans 15g, and pintos 12g.
- *Grains.* Quinoa is queen with 9g per cup, while brown rice has 5g; barley has 3.5g per cup as well.
- *Best bet.* Combine different protein-rich foods to get the most protein—if you have lentils served over quinoa, you will tally up 27g of protein for the meal! That's more than half of what you'll need if you're a 130-pound woman (the formula is .37 $\times$ body weight = amount of protein. In this case, .37 $\times$ 130 = 48g per day).

CRUSTY TOFU

Serves 6

1 tablespoon paprika
1½ teaspoons chili powder
Salt and pepper to taste
1 (14–16-ounce) package extra-firm tofu
3 tablespoons boiling water
2 tablespoons lemon juice
4 teaspoons honey
1 tablespoon olive oil
3 tablespoons pine nuts, toasted

In a small bowl, mix paprika, chili powder, and salt and pepper. Drain tofu and pat dry with paper towels. Cut crosswise into eight slices about ½-inch thick. Dredge tofu in spice mixture, coating completely.

In a small bowl, mix boiling water, lemon juice, and honey.

In a skillet, heat oil over medium-high heat. Add tofu and cook on one side until brown and crusty, 4 to 5 minutes; flip and cook on other side for another 3 minutes.

Add honey mixture to pan and shake to coat tofu. Serve immediately, topped with toasted pine nuts.

PER SERVING:
123 Calories; 8g Fat; 7g Protein; 8g Carbohydrate; 1g Dietary Fiber; 0mg Cholesterol; 13mg Sodium. Exchanges: 0 Grain (Starch); 1½ Lean Meat; 0 Fruit; 1 Fat; ½ Other Carbohydrates.

SERVING SUGGESTIONS: Serve with corn on the cob and sautéed zucchini with diced tomatoes and garlic.

SOUTHWESTERN BLACK BEANS

Serves 6

1 tablespoon vegetable oil

1 small onion, finely chopped

1 (28-ounce) can black beans

1 teaspoon chipotle chilies in adobo

2 large tomatoes, diced

4 chopped cilantro sprigs

2¼ cups frozen corn kernels (or you can use fresh, about 3 ears)

Salt to taste

In a large skillet, heat oil over medium-high heat; add onion and cook till translucent, about 3 to 4 minutes.

Add beans, chilies, tomatoes, and cilantro; lower heat and simmer 15 to 30 minutes.

In the last 10 minutes, add corn kernels. Season with salt. If too dry, add up to 1 cup of water.

PER SERVING:
249 Calories; 4g Fat; 14g Protein; 43g Carbohydrate; 13g Dietary Fiber; trace Cholesterol; 17mg Sodium. Exchanges: 2½ Grain (Starch); 1 Lean Meat; ½ Vegetable; ½ Fat.

SERVING SUGGESTIONS: Serve with brown rice, shredded Monterey Jack and Cheddar cheeses, and chopped cilantro. Don't forget to add a big green salad!

RASPBERRY SALAD

Serves 6

SALAD

3 cups romaine lettuce, torn into bite-size pieces
1 cup thinly sliced red cabbage
½ cup sliced English cucumber
2 cups raspberries (reserving 2 tablespoons for dressing)
¼ cup dried cranberries
2 tablespoons chopped chives

DRESSING

¾ cup olive oil
⅔ cup red wine vinegar
2–3 tablespoons honey
2 teaspoons Dijon mustard
½ teaspoon dried basil
1 tablespoon minced fresh parsley

In a large bowl, combine salad ingredients. Blend dressing ingredients in blender, including the reserved 2 tablespoons raspberries. Toss greens and berries with dressing and serve immediately.

PER SERVING:
296 Calories; 27g Fat; 1g Protein; 14g Carbohydrate; 4g Dietary Fiber; 0mg Cholesterol; 26mg Sodium. Exchanges: 0 Grain (Starch); 0 Lean Meat; ½ Vegetable; ½ Fruit; 5½ Fat; ½ Other Carbohydrates.

SERVING SUGGESTION: Serve with open-faced melted cheese croissants. Using whole wheat croissants, cut them down the middle, add whatever sliced cheese you have laying around the fridge, and broil the croissants till hot and bubbly. Or skip the broiling and serve croissants with cold sliced cheese if the weather is too hot.

GRILLED VEGETABLE QUESADILLAS

Serves 6

1 medium zucchini, sliced

1 medium yellow summer squash, sliced

1 large red bell pepper, seeded, deribbed, and sliced

1 large onion, sliced

1 cup sliced mushrooms

12 whole wheat tortillas

2 cups shredded low-fat Monterey Jack cheese

1 cup chopped cilantro

Preheat outdoor grill, indoor grill, or broiler.

Combine veggies and grill, using a grilling basket (see sidebar on grilling, page 181).

When veggies are done, arrange them on six of the tortillas. Top with cheese, cilantro, and remaining tortillas. Wrap in foil and set on grill just long enough for cheese to melt. Cut into wedges and serve.

PER SERVING:
281 Calories; 9g Fat; 11g Protein; 40g Carbohydrate; 4g Dietary Fiber; 17mg Cholesterol; 610mg Sodium. Exchanges: ½ Lean Meat; 1 Vegetable; 1 Fat.

SERVING SUGGESTIONS: Serve with sour cream, your favorite jarred salsa, and a big green salad.

DO AHEAD TIP: Cook lentils for tomorrow night's meal.

ANOTHER NUTTY LENTIL LOAF

Serves 6

1 tablespoon vegetable oil
1 large onion, finely chopped
2 celery stalks, diced
2 cups shredded carrots
1 red bell pepper, seeded, deribbed, and diced
2 garlic cloves, pressed
1 tablespoon cumin
Salt and pepper to taste
2 cups brown lentils, drained and rinsed
3 cups shredded Cheddar cheese
1 cup coarsely chopped cashews
3 eggs, beaten

In a large skillet, heat oil over medium-high heat. Add onion and celery and cook until celery softens, about 5 minutes. Add carrots, bell pepper, garlic, and cumin and stir for another 2 minutes. Season with salt and pepper. Remove from heat and set aside.

In a large mixing bowl, combine lentils, cheese, and cashews. Add veggies from skillet and stir well. Add eggs and mix until blended. Add salt and pepper to taste. Spoon into a greased casserole dish that will fit in your slow cooker and cover tightly with foil.

Place in slow cooker and add enough boiling water to come 1 inch up the sides. Cover and cook on high for 4 to 5 hours, until loaf has set.

PER SERVING:
524 Calories; 35g Fat; 28g Protein; 29g Carbohydrate; 9g Dietary Fiber; 165mg Cholesterol; 420mg Sodium. Exchanges: 1½ Grain (Starch); 3 Lean Meat; 1½ Vegetable; 5 Fat.

SERVING SUGGESTIONS: Serve with stuffed broiled tomatoes (cut tomatoes in half so they stand up well, stuff with cheese and bread crumbs (half shredded cheese, half seasoned bread crumbs), top with more bread crumbs, and broil till tops are browned. Add steamed broccoli for a colorful meal.

✳ Week Three

DAY ONE: Heavenly Pasta and Vegetables

DAY TWO: Beany Tofu Barbecue

DAY THREE: Tortilla Pizzas

DAY FOUR: Veggie Supreme Sandwiches

DAY FIVE: Savory Summer Stir-Fry

DAY SIX: Barbecued Lima Beans

SHOPPING LIST

CONDIMENTS

Olive oil

Barbecue sauce, your choice

Italian dressing

Ketchup

Tabasco sauce

Dark corn syrup

**Mayonnaise

**Rice vinegar (1 meal)

**Salsa, your favorite (1 meal)

**Vinegar or apple cider

DELI

**Potato salad (or make homemade; see page 255)

PRODUCE

1 (14–16-ounce) package firm tofu

3 pounds yellow onions (keep on hand)

1 Vidalia onion

1 garlic head

1 small red bell pepper

8 mushrooms

3 large zucchini

8 tomatoes (5 medium, 3 large); **additional (1 meal)

6 leaves lettuce (see note on spinach)

2 avocadoes; **additional (1 meal)

1 small cucumber

1 slice ginger root

1 bunch parsley

1 peach

**Fresh basil (1 meal)

**Green onions (1 meal)

**Baby carrots (1 meal)

**Coleslaw mix (2 meals)

**Cilantro (1 meal)

**Lettuce, not iceberg (1 meal)

**Salad toppings (1 meal)

**Spinach (can be used in place of 6 lettuce leaves, or in addition to them)

**Celery

**Potatoes

CANNED GOODS

1 (14.5-ounce) can low-sodium vegetable broth

1 (14.5-ounce) can whole tomatoes

1 (14.5-ounce) can diced tomatoes

1 (15-ounce) can chickpeas

2 (15-ounce) cans black beans; **additional 1 can (1 meal)

**1 (15-ounce) can white beans (1 meal)

DAIRY/DAIRY CASE

Grated Parmesan cheese (3 tablespoons)

Shredded mozzarella cheese (2 cups); **additional (slices; 1 meal)

8 ounces chives and onion-flavored cream cheese

**Sour cream

DRY GOODS
Brown sugar

Angel hair pasta (12 ounces)

Brown rice (3 cups)

1 pound dried lima beans

BREADS/BAKERY
6 whole wheat buns

12 slices whole wheat bread

6 flour tortillas

**Cornbread (1 meal)

FROZEN FOODS
1 (16-ounce) package frozen broccoli, cauliflower, and
carrots medley

Serves 6

12 ounces angel hair pasta

1 teaspoon olive oil

¼ cup chopped onion

1 small red bell pepper, seeded, deribbed, and diced

1 garlic clove, pressed

1 (14.5-ounce) can whole tomatoes

1 (16-ounce) package frozen broccoli, cauliflower, and carrots medley

3 tablespoons grated Parmesan cheese

Cook pasta according to package directions until al dente; drain and keep warm.

In a large skillet, heat oil over medium heat. Add onion, bell pepper, and garlic and cook for 3 minutes. Stir in tomatoes and frozen vegetables. Break up tomatoes with a spoon, cover, and cook for 8 minutes.

Heap pasta onto a large platter and spoon tomato-vegetable mixture into center. Sprinkle with Parmesan cheese.

PER SERVING:
270 Calories; 3g Fat; 11g Protein; 51g Carbohydrate; 5g Dietary Fiber; 2mg Cholesterol; 171mg Sodium. Exchanges: 3 Grain (Starch); 0 Lean Meat; 1½ Vegetable; ½ Fat.

SERVING SUGGESTION: Serve with Caprese Salad (see page 111).

BEANY TOFU BARBECUE

4 garlic cloves, pressed
1 onion, chopped
2 teaspoons olive oil
1 (16–18-ounce) bottle barbecue sauce
1 (14.5-ounce) can diced tomatoes
1 (15-ounce) can chickpeas, drained
1 (14–16-ounce) package firm tofu, drained and cubed
6 whole wheat buns

In a large skillet, sauté garlic and onion in oil over medium heat until onion is translucent, about 3 to 4 minutes.

Stir in barbecue sauce and diced tomatoes. Next add chickpeas and tofu. Stir and continue to cook till heated through. Serve on whole wheat buns.

PER SERVING:
377 Calories; 9g Fat; 17g Protein; 57g Carbohydrate; 8g Dietary Fiber; 0mg Cholesterol; 1117mg Sodium. Exchanges: 3 Grain (Starch); 1½ Lean Meat; 1 Vegetable; 1 Fat; ½ Other Carbohydrates.

SERVING SUGGESTIONS: Serve with coleslaw and a bowl of baby carrots.

TORTILLA PIZZAS

Serves 6

"This was a hit at our house for both the adults *and* the kids!"

—Suzyn F.

6 flour tortillas
2 (15-ounce) cans black beans, rinsed and drained
2 cups shredded mozzarella cheese
1 large onion, chopped
5 ripe medium tomatoes, thinly sliced

Preheat broiler. Lay out tortillas on a large baking sheet. Spoon ½ cup of black beans onto each tortilla, mashing lightly with the back of the spoon.

Sprinkle ¼ cup cheese over each tortilla. Top with onion and tomato slices, and then sprinkle with remaining cheese.

Broil for 3 to 4 minutes or until the cheese melts. (If the house is too hot for that, you could also heat in a skillet over medium heat for 4 to 5 minutes.)

PER SERVING:
503 Calories; 16g Fat; 23g Protein; 66g Carbohydrate; 11g Dietary Fiber; 34mg Cholesterol; 947mg Sodium. Exchanges: 4 Grain (Starch); 1½ Lean Meat; 1 Vegetable; 2 Fat.

SERVING SUGGESTIONS: Serve with some condiments on the side: chopped cilantro, your favorite salsa, sour cream, and sliced avocado. Add a big salad and you've got dinner!

Smooth Operator

Smoothies are great for breakfast, an easy snack, or can even be frozen for a simple dessert! Here are some general guidelines for making awesome smoothies. My rule of thumb is to use what I have on hand in the fruit department.

Makes 1 serving.

2 ounces silkened tofu
1 very ripe banana, peeled and frozen
¼ cup berries, frozen (see below)
1 scoop protein powder
1 teaspoon vanilla extract
⅓ cup orange juice

Having the fruit frozen makes your smoothie a creamy, dreamy milk shake. Simply put everything in a blender and let 'er rip! For the berries option, you could use peaches, some more banana, whatever. Smoothies are pretty forgiving—the only necessary component is frozen fruit to make it shake-like. If you have a muffin and smoothie for breakfast, you're set to go till lunch.

Here are some general smoothie rules to make your very own signature smoothie:

- *Something sweet.* This is the place to use those overly ripe bananas. Peel and freeze them and you've got your base.
- *Something extra.* Whatever you want—frozen berries, fruit, orange juice concentrate—this is the flavoring component. You can always just add more banana too, for a banana smoothie.
- *Something liquid.* Soy milk, dairy milk, or even rice milk. This adds the creamy factor and turns an ordinary smoothie into a sensual experience.
- *Something more.* To add more protein, use a protein powder from the health food store. With everything you have going on in your smoothie, there is no way you'll taste it.

VEGGIE SUPREME SANDWICHES

Serves 6

"A really good sandwich. A perfect summer meal!"   —Suzyn F.

> 1 (8-ounce) container chives and onion-flavored cream cheese
> 12 slices whole wheat bread
> 6 green leaf lettuce leaves
> 1 large onion, thinly sliced
> 1 large tomato, thinly sliced
> 2 ripe avocados, peeled and sliced
> 1 small cucumber, thinly sliced
> ¼ cup Italian dressing

Spread a thin layer of cream cheese on one side of each slice of bread.

Arrange lettuce and the rest of the veggies on six slices. Drizzle dressing over vegetables and top with remaining six bread slices.

PER SERVING:
436 Calories; 29g Fat; 10g Protein; 38g Carbohydrate; 7g Dietary Fiber; 38mg Cholesterol; 522mg Sodium. Exchanges: 1½ Grain (Starch); ½ Lean Meat; 1 Vegetable; ½ Fruit; 5½ Fat; 0 Other Carbohydrates.

SERVING SUGGESTION: Serve with potato salad, either homemade (see page 255) or from the deli. To boost the nutrition in this sandwich, substitute baby spinach for the lettuce or just add it in.

SAVORY SUMMER STIR-FRY

Serves 6

> 3 tablespoons olive oil
> ½ Vidalia onion, chopped
> ½ teaspoon minced ginger root
> 3 garlic cloves, pressed
> 2 teaspoons chopped fresh parsley
> 8 mushrooms, cleaned and thinly sliced
> 3 large zucchini, sliced in circles
> 2 large tomatoes, chopped
> 1 peach, skinned, pitted, and chopped into large pieces
> 1 teaspoon brown sugar
> Salt and pepper to taste
> 6 cups cooked brown rice

In a large skillet, heat 2 tablespoons olive oil over medium-high heat. Add onion, ginger, garlic, and parsley. Sauté over medium heat until vegetables are browned, about 3 to 4 minutes.

Add mushrooms and sauté about 5 minutes. Add zucchini, tomatoes, peach, brown sugar, and salt and pepper along with the remaining tablespoon of oil.

Cover and let simmer 15 to 20 minutes, stirring occasionally, until tender. Serve over brown rice.

PER SERVING:
324 Calories; 9g Fat; 7g Protein; 56g Carbohydrate; 6g Dietary Fiber; 0mg Cholesterol; 11mg Sodium. Exchanges: 3 Grain (Starch); 1½ Vegetable; 0 Fruit; 1½ Fat; 0 Other Carbohydrates.

SERVING SUGGESTION: Serve with a black and white bean salad (mix in a large bowl a rinsed can of black beans and white beans, toss together with Italian salad dressing, and garnish with chopped green onions).

DO AHEAD TIP: Soak lima beans overnight for tomorrow's dinner.

BARBECUED LIMA BEANS

1 pound dried lima beans, picked over and washed
3½ cups water
1½ cups chopped onion
½ cup brown sugar
½ cup ketchup
8 drops Tabasco sauce
⅓ cup dark corn syrup
1 (14.5-ounce) can low-sodium vegetable broth
Salt and pepper to taste

In a large saucepan, soak beans in water overnight. Do not drain.

Add onion to beans and bring to a boil. Simmer 30 to 60 minutes or until beans are beginning to get tender. Drain beans.

Combine beans, onion, brown sugar, ketchup, tabasco, and corn syrup in slow cooker. Mix well. Pour in vegetable broth to cover beans. If you need more liquid, add water until beans are barely covered. Add salt and pepper. Cover and cook on low for 10 hours or on high for 4 to 6 hours, stirring occasionally.

PER SERVING:
402 Calories; 1g Fat; 20g Protein; 83g Carbohydrate; 16g Dietary Fiber; 0mg Cholesterol; 427mg Sodium. Exchanges: 3 Grain (Starch); 1 Lean Meat; ½ Vegetable; 2 Other Carbohydrates.

SERVING SUGGESTIONS: Serve with coleslaw and cornbread for a hearty meal.

✳ Week Four

DAY ONE: Couscous with Verdant Veggies

DAY TWO: Marinated Tofu with Veggies

DAY THREE: Beanburgers

DAY FOUR: Taco Salad

DAY FIVE: Orzo-and-Corn-Filled Tomatoes

DAY SIX: Mushroom Lasagna

SHOPPING LIST

CONDIMENTS

Vegetable oil

Olive oil

Vinegar (if using white grape juice)

Dry white wine (if not using white grape juice)

White grape juice (if not using white wine)

Ketchup

Salsa, your favorite

Apple juice

**Salad dressing, your favorite (3 meals)

**Poppy seed dressing (1 meal)

**Burger toppings (mustard, ketchup, mayo, relish, etc.;
   1 meal)

DELI

**Potato salad (or make homemade; see page 255)
   (1 meal)

PRODUCE

1 (14–16-ounce) package firm tofu

3 pounds yellow onions (keep on hand)

1 bunch green onions

1 garlic head

1 bunch celery

2 (8-ounce) cartons mushrooms

1 medium cucumber

1 bundle asparagus

4 ounces snow peas

1 head green lettuce; **additional (1 meal)

8 tomatoes (2 medium, 6 large); **additional (1 meal)

4 lemons

2 cups arugula leaves

1 bunch mint

1 bunch thyme

1 bunch basil

1 bunch parsley

**Strawberries (2 meals)

**Raspberries (1 meal)

**Blueberries (1 meal)

**Peaches (1 meal)

**Spinach (2 meals)

**Lettuce, not iceberg (1 meal)

**Salad toppings (3 meals)

**Red onion (1 meal)

**Baby carrots (1 meal)

**Russet potatoes (1 meal)

CANNED GOODS

2 (14.5-ounce) cans low-sodium vegetable broth

4 (15-ounce) cans red kidney beans

1 (15-ounce) can Mexican-style corn

3 (8-ounce) cans tomato sauce

SPICES AND DRIED HERBS

Oregano

Thyme

Sage

Garlic powder

1 (1.25-ounce) package taco seasoning mix

DAIRY/DAIRY CASE

Eggs (1)

Diced Monterey Jack cheese (1 cup)

Cottage cheese (2 cups)

Shredded Cheddar cheese (2 cups)

Sour cream; **additional (1 meal)

Grated Parmesan cheese (½ cup)

Grated mozzarella cheese (2 cups)

**Vanilla yogurt (1 meal)

**Cheese slices, your choice (1 meal)

**Blend of shredded Cheddar/Jack cheese (1 cup)

DRY GOODS

Cornstarch

Lasagna noodles (12)

Orzo (4 ounces)

Couscous (1½ cups)

Seasoned bread crumbs (½ cup)

TVP crumbles (12 ounces)

Pine nuts (3 tablespoons)

Tortilla chips (9 ounces)

BREADS/BAKERY

**Garlic bread (1 meal)

**Whole wheat tortillas

FROZEN FOODS

1 (16-ounce) package frozen corn kernels

COUSCOUS WITH VERDANT VEGGIES

1 lemon
5 tablespoons olive oil
Salt and pepper to taste
2 cups arugula leaves, gently packed
½ medium cucumber, halved lengthwise and sliced
3 tablespoons chopped fresh mint
2 cups low-sodium vegetable broth
1½ cups couscous
3 tablespoons pine nuts, toasted

In a medium bowl, squeeze juice from 1 lemon. Whisk in 4 tablespoons of oil on a slow, steady stream until well blended. Add salt and pepper. Stir in arugula, cucumber, and mint. Set aside.

In a small saucepan, bring broth to a boil. Set aside.

In a medium saucepan, heat remaining tablespoon of oil over medium heat. Stir in couscous, making sure oil coats it. Add hot broth and salt to taste. Allow mixture to come to a vigorous simmer, stirring frequently. Remove from heat, cover, and let stand till liquid is absorbed, about 8 minutes.

Fluff with a fork and then add arugula mixture. Cover and let stand until the arugula wilts, 2 to 3 minutes. Serve sprinkled with pine nuts.

PER SERVING:
311 Calories; 14g Fat; 11g Protein; 37g Carbohydrate; 4g Dietary Fiber; 0mg Cholesterol; 180mg Sodium. Exchanges: 2 Grain (Starch); ½ Lean Meat; ½ Vegetable; 0 Fruit; 2½ Fat.

SERVING SUGGESTION: Serve with Berry-Peach Fruit Salad: put fresh berries (strawberries, raspberries, blueberries) and diced fresh peaches in individual bowls, gently toss together, and top with a dollop of vanilla yogurt.

MARINATED TOFU WITH VEGGIES

Serves 6

1 pound firm tofu, drained and cut into ½-inch cubes
2 garlic cloves, pressed
2 tablespoons finely chopped fresh thyme
4 tablespoons olive oil
Salt and pepper to taste
2 green onions, thinly sliced
8 ounces mushrooms, cleaned and thinly sliced
1 bundle asparagus, cut into 1-inch lengths
4 ounces snow peas, cut in half diagonally
⅔ cup dry white wine (or use white grape juice with a splash of vinegar)
⅔ cup low-sodium vegetable broth
1 tablespoon cornstarch

In a bowl, combine drained and cubed tofu, garlic, thyme, 1 tablespoon oil, and salt and pepper. Cover and let stand for 20 minutes.

To a large heated skillet, add tofu and marinade and cook till lightly browned, about 4 to 5 minutes. Transfer to a plate.

In the same skillet, heat remaining 3 tablespoons oil and add green onions. Cook for 3 to 4 minutes. Add mushrooms and cook another 2 minutes. Next add asparagus and snow peas, and cook for 2 minutes. Pour in wine and vegetable broth.

In a measuring cup, blend cornstarch with 2 tablespoons water; add water to make ⅓ cup. Pour cornstarch mixture into skillet, bring to a boil, and continue to cook until veggies are tender, about 2 to 3 minutes more. Add salt and pepper to taste. Sprinkle tofu over the top.

PER SERVING:
200 Calories; 13g Fat; 8g Protein; 11g Carbohydrate; 2g Dietary Fiber; trace Cholesterol; 191mg Sodium. Exchanges: ½ Grain (Starch); 1½ Lean Meat; 1 Vegetable; 2½ Fat.

SERVING SUGGESTIONS: Serve with a big spinach salad and a bowl of baby carrots for the table.

BEANBURGERS

3 (15-ounce) cans red kidney beans, drained and rinsed
1 large egg
½ cup seasoned bread crumbs
2 tablespoons ketchup
½ teaspoon garlic powder
1 teaspoon dried oregano
⅛ teaspoon dried thyme
¼ teaspoon dried sage
¼ cup finely chopped onion
3 tablespoons vegetable oil
Salt and pepper to taste

In a large bowl, combine beans, egg, bread crumbs, ketchup, garlic powder, oregano, thyme, sage, and onion. Using a fork or potato masher, mash until most of the beans are squished (or process in food processor using the on/off option). With wet hands, shape the mixture into six ½-inch-thick patties.

In a large skillet, heat oil over medium-high heat. Add patties and cook for 3 to 4 minutes on each side, or until browned and crisp. Salt and pepper to taste.

PER SERVING:
239 Calories; 2g Fat; 14g Protein; 43g Carbohydrate; 14g Dietary Fiber; 36mg Cholesterol; 1061mg Sodium. Exchanges: 2½ Grain (Starch); ½ Lean Meat; 0 Vegetable; 0 Fat; 0 Other Carbohydrates.

SERVING SUGGESTIONS: To make Cheesy Beanburgers, after cooking, keep burgers in skillet and reduce heat to low. Top each patty with cheese. Cover and cook for 1 to 2 minutes, till the cheese melts. Add a delicious potato salad and the usual fixin's for burgers, like lettuce, tomato, sliced onion, mustard, ketchup, and mayo.

TACO SALAD

1 (12-ounce) bag TVP crumbles
1¾ cups salsa
2 garlic cloves, pressed
1 (1.25-ounce) package taco seasoning mix
1 (15-ounce) can Mexican-style corn
1 (15-ounce) can red kidney beans
9 ounces tortilla chips
1 medium head green leaf lettuce
2 cups shredded Cheddar cheese
2 medium tomatoes, chopped
Sour cream

In a large skillet, brown TVP crumbles and drain. Stir in 1 cup salsa, garlic, seasoning mix, corn, and beans. Remove from heat and slightly cool.

In a large serving bowl, layer half each of tortilla chips, meat mixture, lettuce, cheese, and tomatoes; repeat layers. Serve immediately with remaining salsa and sour cream.

PER SERVING:
704 Calories; 27g Fat; 57g Protein; 73g Carbohydrate; 22g Dietary Fiber; 40mg Cholesterol; 1555mg Sodium. Exchanges: 4½ Grain (Starch); 6½ Lean Meat; 1 Vegetable; 4 Fat; 0 Other Carbohydrates.

SERVING SUGGESTION: Serve with quesadillas—shredded cheese (I like a blend of Monterey Jack and Cheddar) sandwiched in whole wheat tortillas (see page 258).

ORZO-AND-CORN-FILLED TOMATOES

Serves 6

3 quarts water
½ cup orzo
3 strips lemon zest
2 cups frozen corn kernels, thawed
1 cup diced Monterey Jack cheese
2 green onions, sliced
⅔ cup chopped celery
2 tablespoons chopped fresh basil
¼ cup apple juice
2 tablespoons lemon juice
2 tablespoons olive oil
Salt and pepper to taste
6 large tomatoes

In a large saucepan, bring water to a boil. Add orzo and lemon zest, and cook for 8 minutes or till orzo is tender but still firm to bite. Drain. Rinse with cold water and drain again. Discard the lemon zest.

In a large bowl, combine orzo, corn, cheese, green onions, celery, basil, apple juice, lemon juice, oil, and salt and pepper.

If necessary, trim the bottoms off tomatoes so they will sit upright. Cut off tops and remove cores. Dice the tomato trimmings and add to the orzo salad (except the inedible green stem). Scoop out the tomato pulp and discard. Invert tomatoes onto a plate lined with paper towels to let them drain.

Fill each tomato with about ½ cup orzo salad. To serve, place each stuffed tomato on a plate and add about 1 cup of orzo salad around the base of tomato. Serve cold or at room temperature.

PER SERVING:
258 Calories; 11g Fat; 10g Protein; 32g Carbohydrate; 3g Dietary Fiber; 17mg Cholesterol; 139mg Sodium. Exchanges: 1½ Grain (Starch); ½ Lean Meat; 1 Vegetable; 0 Fruit; 1½ Fat.

SERVING SUGGESTIONS: Serve with a big spinach salad. Add sliced strawberries and thinly sliced red onion, and toss together with a poppy seed dressing (you can make or purchase).

MUSHROOM LASAGNA

Serves 6

1 tablespoon olive oil
1 (8-ounce) carton mushrooms
2 garlic cloves, pressed
2 tablespoons fresh chopped parsley
Salt and pepper to taste
1 tablespoon lemon juice
3 cups tomato sauce
12 lasagna noodles
2 cups cottage cheese
½ cup grated Parmesan cheese
2 cups grated mozzarella cheese

In a skillet, heat oil over medium heat. Add mushrooms and cook till their liquid begins to be released, about 4 to 5 minutes. Add garlic and parsley, and cook for another minute. Remove from heat and stir in salt and pepper and lemon juice. Set aside.

In the bottom of a slow cooker, spread one-fourth of tomato sauce. Cover with four noodles, breaking them if need be to fit. Spread with half the cottage cheese, half the mushroom mixture, and one-third each of the Parmesan and mozzarella cheeses. Repeat. Arrange the last layer of noodles over cheeses. Pour remaining sauce over top and sprinkle with remaining Parmesan and mozzarella cheeses. Cover and cook on low for 8 hours or on high for 4 hours.

PER SERVING:
427 Calories; 16g Fat; 29g Protein; 43g Carbohydrate; 3g Dietary Fiber; 45mg Cholesterol; 1333mg Sodium. Exchanges: 2 Grain (Starch); 3 Lean Meat; 2 Vegetable; 0 Fruit; 2 Fat.

SERVING SUGGESTIONS: A big green salad and garlic bread will round this lovely lasagna off nicely.

✳ Week Five

DAY ONE: Greek Tortellini

DAY TWO: Veggie and Noodle Stir-Fry with Tofu

DAY THREE: Wilted Spinach and White Beans

DAY FOUR: Crunchy Lentil Salad

DAY FIVE: Sloppy Joes

DAY SIX: Crock Italian Mushrooms

SHOPPING LIST

CONDIMENTS

Olive oil

Vegetable oil

White vinegar

Balsamic vinegar

Soy sauce, low-sodium if available

Chili sauce (½ cup)

Prepared mustard

1 (2.25-ounce) can black olives

**Salad dressing, your choice (2 meals)

**Hummus (or make homemade, page 259; 1 meal)

**Mayonnaise

**Rice vinegar

PRODUCE

1 (14–16-ounce) package firm tofu

3 pounds yellow onions (keep on hand)

1 red onion

3 garlic heads

5 large green bell peppers

1 bunch celery

2 (8-ounce) cartons oyster or button mushrooms

2 carrots

2 pounds tomatoes

12 ounces snow peas

2 large yellow summer squash

12 cups baby spinach

1-inch piece ginger root

1 bunch parsley

1 bunch basil

2 lemons (for 3 tablespoons juice)

**Lettuce, not iceberg (2 meals)

**Salad toppings (2 meals)

**Coleslaw mix (1 meal)

**Broccoli florets (1 meal)

**Broccoli (1 meal)

**Cauliflower florets (1 meal)

**Grape tomatoes (1 meal)

**Baby carrots (2 meals)

CANNED GOODS

2 (14.5-ounce) cans low-sodium vegetable broth

3 (14.5-ounce) cans diced tomatoes

2 (16-ounce) cans white kidney beans

1 (8-ounce) can tomato sauce

SPICES AND DRIED HERBS

Marjoram

Oregano

Bay leaves

Cumin

Garlic salt

DAIRY/DAIRY CASE

Cheese-filled tortellini (2 9-ounce packages)

Crumbled feta cheese (with sun-dried tomatoes, if you can find it) (½ cup)

**Shredded cheese, your choice (Cheddar/Jack blend recommended) (1 meal)

DRY GOODS

Cornstarch

Brown sugar

Fettuccini pasta (12 ounces)

Brown rice (3 cups); **additional (1 meal)

Lentils (1½ cups)

TVP crumbles (3 cups)

BREADS/BAKERY

**6 hamburger buns or 12 slices bread (1 meal)

**Pita bread (2 meals)

GREEK TORTELLINI

1 pound ripe tomatoes, seeded and chopped
1 (2.25-ounce) can black olives, drained
3 garlic cloves, pressed
½ cup chopped fresh basil
¼ cup olive oil
3 tablespoons balsamic vinegar
Salt and pepper to taste
2 (9-ounce) packages refrigerated cheese-filled tortellini
½ cup crumbled feta cheese with sun-dried tomatoes

In a serving bowl, combine everything except pasta and cheese. Cook tortellini according to package directions and drain. Add tortellini to tomato mixture and gently toss. Sprinkle with cheese. Serve warm or cold.

PER SERVING:
375 Calories; 18g Fat; 15g Protein; 39g Carbohydrate; 3g Dietary Fiber; 69mg Cholesterol; 567mg Sodium. Exchanges: 2 Grain (Starch); 1 Lean Meat; ½ Vegetable; 0 Fruit; 3 Fat.

SERVING SUGGESTIONS: Serve with a big green salad and pita bread triangles with hummus (purchased or homemade, see page 259).

VEGGIE AND NOODLE
STIR-FRY WITH TOFU

Serves 6

12 ounces fettuccine
1½ cups low-sodium vegetable broth
½ cup low-sodium soy sauce
2 tablespoons cornstarch
1½ tablespoons vegetable oil
¾ pound snow peas, stringed
2 large yellow summer squash, cut into ¼-inch slices
1½ large green bell peppers, seeded, deribbed, and chopped
3 garlic cloves, pressed
1-inch piece grated ginger root
12 ounces firm tofu, cut into ½-inch pieces
Salt and pepper to taste

Cook pasta according to package directions until al dente. Drain, reserving 1 cup of cooking water.

In a small bowl, stir together broth, soy sauce, and cornstarch.

In a deep skillet, heat oil over high heat. Add vegetables, garlic, and ginger; cook for 3 to 4 minutes. Add the tofu and cook for 2 more minutes, until heated through.

Give cornstarch mixture a quick re-stir and add to skillet. Cook, stirring constantly, for 2 more minutes, until sauce thickens and bubbles. Salt and pepper to taste. Remove from heat and keep warm.

Mix vegetable stir-fry into pasta, adding some of the reserved cooking water if needed. Toss well.

PER SERVING:
393 Calories; 8g Fat; 17g Protein; 64g Carbohydrate; 6g Dietary Fiber; 1mg Cholesterol; 1219mg Sodium. Exchanges: 3½ Grain (Starch); 1 Lean Meat; 2 Vegetable; 1 Fat.

SERVING SUGGESTION: A big green salad is all you need with this rich meal.

WILTED SPINACH AND WHITE BEANS

Serves 6

¾ cup low-sodium vegetable broth

4 garlic cloves, pressed

12 cups baby spinach

Salt and pepper to taste

2 (16-ounce) cans white kidney beans, rinsed and drained

2 cups coarsely chopped tomatoes

1½ tablespoons olive oil

In a large skillet, bring broth and garlic to a boil over high heat. Reduce heat to low, cover, and simmer for 4 to 5 minutes, or till the garlic is soft.

Add spinach and salt and pepper. Cover and cook over medium-high heat, stirring often, for 2 to 4 minutes, till the spinach is wilted.

Add the beans and tomatoes. Stir for a minute till heated through. Remove pan from heat. Stir in olive oil and serve immediately.

PER SERVING:
342 Calories; 5g Fat; 25g Protein; 55g Carbohydrate; 19g Dietary Fiber; 0mg Cholesterol; 119mg Sodium. Exchanges: 2½ Grain (Starch); 1 Lean Meat; 3 Vegetable; ½ Fat.

SERVING SUGGESTIONS: Serve on a bed of brown rice and add a nice relish tray for the table: broccoli and cauliflower florets, grape tomatoes, baby carrots, whatever else you like.

CRUNCHY LENTIL SALAD

1½ cup lentils, rinsed
7½ cups water
1 bay leaf
2 celery stalks, finely chopped
2 carrots, finely chopped
½ cup finely chopped red onion
3 tablespoons finely chopped fresh parsley
½ cup olive oil
3 tablespoons fresh lemon juice
2 garlic cloves, pressed
½ teaspoon dried marjoram
½ teaspoon cumin
Salt and pepper to taste

In a medium saucepan, combine lentils, water, and bay leaf. Bring to a boil and cook, uncovered, stirring occasionally, for about 15 minutes or till lentils are tender but still crunchy. Drain well, discarding the bay leaf. Let set for about 5 minutes to make sure all the water disappears.

In a serving bowl, combine lentils, celery, carrots, onion, and parsley, gently stirring.

In a small mixing bowl, combine olive oil, lemon juice, garlic, marjoram, cumin, and salt and pepper. Pour over lentil mixture and carefully toss. Serve at room temperature.

PER SERVING:
344 Calories; 19g Fat; 14g Protein; 33g Carbohydrate; 16g Dietary Fiber; 0mg Cholesterol; 36mg Sodium. Exchanges: 2 Grain (Starch); 1 Lean Meat; 1 Vegetable; 0 Fruit; 3½ Fat.

SERVING SUGGESTION: Serve with open-faced melted pitas. Open a whole-grain pita bread, spread a shredded cheese blend (I like Cheddar and Jack), and broil.

SLOPPY JOES

Serves 6

1 cup boiling water
3 cups TVP crumbles
1 cup boiling water
¾ cup finely chopped onion
1½ teaspoons garlic salt
Pepper to taste
½ cup chili sauce
¼ cup brown sugar
1 tablespoon white vinegar
1 tablespoon prepared mustard
1 (8-ounce) can tomato sauce
6 hamburger buns or 12 slices bread, toasted

In a large bowl, pour the boiling water over the TVP and set aside for 10 to 15 minutes.

In a large skillet, sauté onion until translucent, about 3 to 4 minutes. Add garlic salt, pepper, chili sauce, brown sugar, vinegar, mustard, and tomato sauce. Stir and simmer for 5 minutes.

Add TVP to saucepan and stir together. Simmer on medium-low heat for another 20 to 30 minutes. Serve over toast or on buns.

PER SERVING:
402 Calories; 1g Fat; 78g Protein; 36g Carbohydrate; 23g Dietary Fiber; 0mg Cholesterol; 812mg Sodium. Exchanges: 1½ Grain (Starch); 1½ Lean Meat; 1 Vegetable; 0 Fat; ½ Other Carbohydrates.

SERVING SUGGESTIONS: Serve with coleslaw and a bowl of baby carrots.

CROCK ITALIAN MUSHROOMS

Serves 6

2 very large onions, chopped

3 large bell peppers, seeded, deribbed, and chopped

3 tablespoons vegetable oil

2 (8-ounce) cartons oyster or button mushrooms, cleaned and sliced

6 garlic cloves, pressed

3 bay leaves

2 teaspoons dried oregano

12 fresh chopped basil leaves

Salt and pepper to taste

3 (14.5-ounce) cans diced tomatoes

6 cups cooked brown rice

In a skillet, sauté onions and peppers in oil until soft, about 4 to 5 minutes. Stir in mushrooms and garlic and cook until mushrooms begin to brown, about 4 to 5 minutes. Pour into slow cooker.

Add remaining ingredients except rice. Stir well. Cover. Cook on low for 4 to 6 hours. Serve over bed of brown rice.

PER SERVING:
380 Calories; 10g Fat; 9g Protein; 68g Carbohydrate; 9g Dietary Fiber; 0mg Cholesterol; 27mg Sodium. Exchanges: 3 Grain (Starch); 4 Vegetable; 1½ Fat.

SERVING SUGGESTION: Serve with steamed broccoli on the side.

✳ Week Six

DAY ONE: Mediterranean Orzo Salad

DAY TWO: Grilled Vegetable Salad

DAY THREE: Black-eyed Peas 'n Peaches Salad

DAY FOUR: Crusty Veggie Sandwiches

DAY FIVE: Tempeh and Green Bean Stir-Fry

DAY SIX: Wild Rice Medley

SHOPPING LIST

CONDIMENTS

Olive oil

Vegetable oil

Balsamic vinegar

Mayonnaise

Italian salad dressing

Honey mustard

Fruit chutney (try the spicy mango!) (often found near relishes)

Kalamata olives (15)

**Honey (1 meal)

**Rice vinegar (1 meal)

**Salad dressing, your favorite (1 meal)

PRODUCE

1 (14–16-ounce) package firm tofu

2 (8-ounce) packages tempeh (near the tofu in the produce area)

3 pounds yellow onions (keep on hand)

2 small red onions; **additional (1 meal)

1–2 bunches green onions

2 garlic heads; **additional

5 green bell peppers

1 bunch celery

12 ounces mushrooms

24 ounces green beans

2 medium zucchini

6 yellow summer squash

1 large cucumber

3 avocados; **additional (1 meal)

3 tomatoes (2 medium, 1 large); **additional (1 meal)

Spinach leaves

2 heads romaine lettuce

1 bunch dill

1–2 lemons (for 2 tablespoons juice)

2 large peaches

**Fresh basil (1 meal)

**Cilantro (1 meal)

**Coleslaw mix (1 meal)

**Red grapes (1 meal)

**Lettuce, not iceberg (1 meal)

**Salad toppings (1 meal)

**Corn on the cob (1 meal)

**Sautéed sugar snap peas (1 meal)

**Grape tomatoes (1 meal)

CANNED GOODS

2 (14.5-ounce) cans low-sodium vegetable broth

2 (14.5-ounce) cans stewed tomatoes

SPICES AND DRIED HERBS

Oregano

Cumin

Crushed red pepper flakes

DAIRY/DAIRY CASE

Butter

Feta cheese (6 ounces)

Grated Parmesan cheese (½ cup)

**Sliced mozzarella cheese (1 meal)

**Blend of shredded Cheddar/Jack cheese, your choice
  (1 meal)

DRY GOODS

Orzo (2¼ cups)

Brown rice (3¾ cups)

Wild rice (¾ cup)

Quick-cooking barley (½ cup)

Quinoa (½ cup)

Dried black-eyed peas (1 cup)

Dried apricot halves (½ cup)

BREADS/BAKERY

12 slices whole wheat bread

**Whole wheat tortillas (1 meal)

**Corn muffins (1 meal)

MEDITERRANEAN ORZO SALAD

Serves 6

Make this salad ahead of time and chill for at least 2 hours.

> 2¼ cups orzo
> 2 medium zucchini, quartered lengthwise and thinly sliced
> 15 Kalamata olives, pitted and sliced
> 6 green onions, thinly sliced
> 2 celery stalks, thinly sliced
> 1 large tomato, seeded and cubed
> 1½ green bell peppers, seeded, deribbed, and chopped
> ½ cup olive oil
> 3 tablespoons balsamic vinegar
> 4 garlic cloves, pressed
> 1½ teaspoons dried oregano
> 1½ tablespoons minced fresh dill
> Salt and pepper to taste
> 6 ounces crumbled feta cheese
> 3 tablespoons mayonnaise

Prepare orzo according to package directions; drain and rinse under cold water. Drain again very thoroughly. Place in a large bowl.

Stir in zucchini, olives, green onions, celery, tomato, and green bell peppers.

In a small bowl, beat together olive oil, vinegar, garlic, oregano, dill, and salt and pepper. Pour over salad and toss to coat well. Sprinkle on the feta cheese and toss again. Add mayonnaise and toss gently. Chill at least 2 hours then bring to room temperature before serving.

PER SERVING:
575 Calories; 34g Fat; 14g Protein; 57g Carbohydrate; 4g Dietary Fiber; 28mg Cholesterol; 528mg Sodium. Exchanges: 3 Grain (Starch); ½ Lean Meat; 1½ Vegetable; 0 Fruit; 5½ Fat.

SERVING SUGGESTION: Serve with Caprese Salad (see page 111).

DO AHEAD TIP: Marinate tofu and vegetables for tomorrow night's meal.

Grilling Tips

One of my very favorite things about hot weather is the incessant use of the barbecue. Or grill, as we call it in the South. Being able to cook everything over an open flame would be wonderful for all seasons, but for most of us, this cooking technique is confined to the summer months. The key is to use the grill in an understanding way so your food is always 'cued to perfection. Here are five easy ways to help you improve your grilling.

1. *Some like it hot.* When using a barbecue, whether gas or charcoal, it is imperative to preheat the grill. You cannot put the food on a cold grill and start that way, for the same reasons you don't stick food in an oven that hasn't been preheated—it messes up the cooking time and the way foods should cook. Don't do it!

2. *Cool tools.* You just might want to check out your favorite hardware store so you can try some fun barbecue implements. There are some wonderful grilling accessories that you just cannot live without. One is a hole-y wok. That's right—big holes in a flat-bottomed wok. I grilled the most incredible stir-fried squash in one of those things. It was easy—sliced zucchini, summer squash, and a little oil and garlic tossed together in the bowl got thrown into that wok, and those vegetables were amazing. Think of the possibilities! I also purchased a flat hole-y cookie sheet–looking thing, and you can cook your veggies or tofu the same way.

3. *More cool tools.* Don't forget when you fire up the barby, you will be needing some good grilling tools. I used to use my kitchen spatula till one day I burned the hair off my arm when I was turning something and that was enough to convince me. Use real grilling tools and spend a few dollars on some nice ones. Lousy tools give you lousy results.

4. *The brush off.* Get a good wire brush to clean the grill, too. Keeping the grill immaculate will improve what you're eating immensely. "Burning off" the old food only works to a degree—you need the brush!

5. *Use marinades.* Marinades infuse themselves into foods and make for a delicious choice for healthy cooking. Marinades also turn even the most mundane veggies and tofu into things exotic and full of flavor.

    To make your own marinades, remember that you need these elements: oil (any type will do, but I prefer a higher-burning oil like sunflower or peanut oil), acid (you can use wine, citrus fruit, or vinegar), and seasonings (the world is wide open on this one—from your own special blend of herbs and spices to soy sauce, and everything in between).

GRILLED VEGETABLE SALAD

Serves 6

1 (14–16-ounce) package firm tofu, drained
¾ cup Italian salad dressing
6 yellow summer squash
2 large green bell peppers, seeded, deribbed, and chopped
1 large onion, chopped
2 cups water
½ cup quinoa
½ cup quick-cooking barley
½ cup shredded spinach leaves

Cut tofu lengthwise into eight slices, about ½-inch thick. In a shallow baking dish, pour ¼ cup of the dressing over the tofu.

In a large, zipper-topped plastic bag, add the vegetables and pour 3 tablespoons of remaining dressing over them. Close bag and gently shake to evenly coat veggies. Chill tofu and veggies for 4 to 24 hours. Cover and refrigerate remaining dressing.

Remove tofu from dressing, discarding dressing. Drain vegetables, reserving dressing. Preheat grill or broiler. Grill vegetables over medium heat for about 6 to 8 minutes. Grill tofu over medium heat for 4 to 6 minutes, turning once or until lightly browned. Remove tofu from grill and cut into triangles. Set aside.

In a large bowl, combine cooked squash and peppers. Add reserved dressing. Toss to coat and set aside.

Meanwhile, in a 2-quart saucepan, bring 2 cups water to a boil. Place quinoa in a fine sieve and rinse under running water. Add quinoa and barley to the pan. Return to boiling; reduce heat. Simmer, covered, for 15 minutes or until water is almost absorbed and grains are tender. Drain.

In a large bowl, gently toss grains with shredded spinach and remaining chilled dressing. Serve grain mixture with vegetables and tofu.

PER SERVING:
346 Calories; 19g Fat; 12g Protein; 36g Carbohydrate; 7g Dietary Fiber; 0mg Cholesterol; 248mg Sodium. Exchanges: 1½ Grain (Starch); 1½ Lean Meat; 2 Vegetable; 0 Fruit; 3½ Fat.

SERVING SUGGESTIONS: Serve with quesadillas (see page 258) and an avocado salad (sliced avocado, chopped red onion, cilantro, and a touch of Italian dressing).

BLACK-EYED PEAS 'N PEACHES SALAD

Serves 6

12 cups salted water

1 cup dried black-eyed peas

1½ heads romaine lettuce, torn into small pieces

2 large ripe peaches, peeled and cut into ½-inch pieces

3 green onions, chopped

¾ cup diced cucumber

2 tablespoons lemon juice

¾ teaspoon cumin

Salt and pepper to taste

In a large stockpot, bring water and black-eyed peas to a boil and simmer 20 minutes, or till tender. Drain peas in a colander and rinse under cold water to cool. Drain well.

In a large bowl, combine black-eyed peas with remaining ingredients. Salad may be chilled for up to 2 hours.

PER SERVING:
142 Calories; 1g Fat; 10g Protein; 26g Carbohydrate; 7g Dietary Fiber; 0mg Cholesterol; 36mg Sodium. Exchanges: 1 Grain (Starch); ½ Lean Meat; 1 Vegetable; ½ Fruit; 0 Fat.

SERVING SUGGESTIONS: Serve with corn muffins and honey butter.

CRUSTY VEGGIE SANDWICHES

Serves 6

½ cup butter, softened
½ cup grated Parmesan cheese
Salt and pepper to taste
12 slices whole wheat bread
4½ tablespoons honey mustard
3 avocados, sliced
2 medium tomatoes, thinly sliced
2 small red onions, sliced
1 green bell pepper, seeded, deribbed, and cut into strips

In a small bowl, blend together butter, Parmesan cheese, and salt and pepper. Spread some of the butter mixture on one side of each slice of bread. In a nonstick skillet over medium-high heat, cook bread slices, buttered side down, for about 3 minutes, till crisp and deep brown. Set aside to cool.

For each sandwich, spread one slice of toast with honey mustard and layer with avocado, tomato, onion, and bell pepper. Place another slice of toast on top.

PER SERVING:
506 Calories; 36g Fat; 11g Protein; 41g Carbohydrate; 6g Dietary Fiber; 47mg Cholesterol; 718mg Sodium. Exchanges: 1½ Grain (Starch); ½ Lean Meat; 1½ Vegetable; ½ Fruit; 7 Fat.

SERVING SUGGESTIONS: Serve with coleslaw and a big bunch of red grapes on the side.

TEMPEH AND GREEN BEAN STIR-FRY

Serves 6

4 tablespoons olive oil

1½ (8-ounce) packages tempeh, sliced in half lengthwise and then
    into thin strips across the width

3 medium onions, chopped

4 garlic cloves, pressed

½ teaspoon crushed red pepper

2¼ teaspoons cumin

1½ pounds green beans, washed, trimmed, and cut in half

1½ (14.5-ounce) cans stewed tomatoes

1 cup water

Salt and pepper to taste

6 cups cooked brown rice

In a skillet, heat 2 tablespoons olive oil over medium-high heat. Add tempeh, putting in just enough to cover the bottom of the pan. Cook until lightly browned, turning over to cook other side, about 4 to 5 minutes. Drain on paper towels.

In a large skillet, heat remaining 2 tablespoons oil over medium-high heat. Sauté onions and garlic for 2 to 3 minutes, until translucent. Add spices and cook for another 2 minutes. Add green beans, tempeh, stewed tomatoes, and water; mix well. Cover, turning heat down to low, and cook for another 5 to 10 minutes depending on how crunchy you like your beans. Salt and pepper to taste. Serve over rice.

PER SERVING:
496 Calories; 15g Fat; 19g Protein; 75g Carbohydrate; 9g Dietary Fiber; 0mg Cholesterol; 42mg Sodium. Exchanges: 3½ Grain (Starch); 1½ Lean Meat; 3½ Vegetable; 2 Fat.

SERVING SUGGESTION: Serve with a big green salad. That's all you need!

WILD RICE MEDLEY

1½ tablespoons vegetable oil

1½ onions, chopped

6 celery stalks, chopped

3 garlic cloves, pressed

¾ cup wild rice

¾ cup brown rice

12 ounces mushrooms, cleaned and sliced

Salt and pepper to taste

3 cups low-sodium vegetable broth

1½ tablespoons balsamic vinegar

½ cup dried apricot halves

6 tablespoons fruit chutney (try spicy mango!)

In a skillet, heat oil over medium heat. Add onions and celery and cook about 5 minutes, until soft. Add garlic and rice, stirring until well mixed. Add mushrooms, and salt and pepper. Add broth and balsamic vinegar and bring to a boil. Transfer to slow cooker. Stir in apricots.

Cover and cook on low for 7 to 8 hours or on high for 4 hours, till rice is tender and liquid has been absorbed. Serve with your favorite fruit chutney.

PER SERVING:
332 Calories; 5g Fat; 13g Protein; 63g Carbohydrate; 7g Dietary Fiber; 0mg Cholesterol; 305mg Sodium. Exchanges: 2 Grain (Starch); ½ Lean Meat; 1½ Vegetable; 1½ Fruit; 1 Fat.

SERVING SUGGESTIONS: Serve with corn on the cob and sautéed sugar snap peas with halved grape tomatoes (I like to sauté mine in olive oil with fresh-pressed garlic, salting and peppering to taste).

FALL

DAY ONE: Bean-Combo Pasta

DAY TWO: Chunky Tomato Soup

DAY THREE: Cajun Bean Confetti

DAY FOUR: Broccoli Sauté

DAY FIVE: Stuffed Peppers with Couscous

DAY SIX: Crock Cauliflower White Chili

SHOPPING LIST

CONDIMENTS

Olive oil

Vegetable oil

Balsamic vinegar

Hot pepper sauce

**Salad dressing, your choice (3 meals)

**Rice vinegar (2 meals)

**Mayonnaise (2 meals)

**Honey (1 meal)

PRODUCE

¾ cup soft silken tofu

3 pounds yellow onions (keep on hand)

1 bunch green onions

3 garlic heads

9 large green bell peppers

1 large red bell pepper

10 medium tomatoes

1 bunch cauliflower

2 bunches broccoli; **additional (1 meal)

1 medium zucchini

1 bunch cilantro

**Lettuce, not iceberg (2 meals)

**Spinach (1 meal)

**Coleslaw mix (1 meal)

**Salad toppings (3 meals)

**Carrots (1 meal)

**Sweet potatoes (1 meal)

CANNED GOODS

5 (14.5-ounce) cans low-sodium vegetable broth

3 (14.5-ounce) cans diced tomatoes

1 (28-ounce) can crushed tomatoes

3 (8-ounce) cans lima beans (if not using frozen)

1 (16-ounce) can chickpeas

2 (14.5-ounce) cans red kidney beans

1 (14.5-ounce) can white kidney beans

3 (8-ounce) cans green beans

1 (4.5-ounce) can chopped green chilies

SPICES AND DRIED HERBS

Oregano

Marjoram

Basil

Thyme

Cumin

Chili powder

Cajun seasoning

Caraway seeds

DAIRY/DAIRY CASE

Shredded Monterey Jack cheese (1½ cups)

Shredded Cheddar cheese (¾ cup)

Feta cheese (9 ounces)

Shredded Pepper Jack cheese (2 cups)

Cream cheese (4 ounces)

**Butter (2 meals)

DRY GOODS

Sugar

Penne pasta (2¼ cups)

Brown rice (3 cups)

1 (9-ounce) package whole wheat couscous

**Raisins (1 meal)

**Walnuts (1 meal)

BREADS/BAKERY

**Garlic bread (1 meal)

**Corn muffins (3 meals)

FROZEN FOODS

1 (16-ounce) package frozen corn kernels

2 (16-ounce) packages frozen lima beans (if not using canned)

BEAN-COMBO PASTA

Serves 6

2¼ cups penne pasta
3 (14.5-ounce) cans diced tomatoes
3 (8-ounce) cans green beans, drained
3 (8.5-ounce) cans lima beans, drained (or use frozen)
2 teaspoons dried thyme
2 garlic cloves, pressed
1½ cups shredded Monterey Jack cheese

Cook the pasta according to package directions until al dente. Drain and keep warm.

In a large skillet, combine tomatoes, green beans, lima beans, thyme, and garlic and bring to a boil. Stir in pasta and cook until heated through. Sprinkle with cheese. Serve immediately.

PER SERVING:
326 Calories; 10g Fat; 17g Protein; 45g Carbohydrate; 9g Dietary Fiber; 25mg Cholesterol; 746mg Sodium. Exchanges: 2 Grain (Starch); 1 Lean Meat; 2½ Vegetable; 1 Fat.

SERVING SUGGESTIONS: Offer a simple salad and garlic bread.

CHUNKY TOMATO SOUP

Serves 6

"Our RAVE from the week was Chunky Tomato Soup. It was a delicious change. Very tasty! About the only way my kids would eat tofu—they didn't even realize it was there and I appreciated the added protein! Thanks!" —Andrea A.

2 tablespoons olive oil
1 large onion, chopped
6 garlic cloves, pressed
1¼ teaspoons dried basil
Salt and pepper to taste
1 (28-ounce) can crushed tomatoes
4 cups low-sodium vegetable broth
2 tablespoons sugar
¾ cup soft silken tofu
6 medium tomatoes, diced (save 2 for garnish)
⅓ cup water
¾ cup shredded Cheddar cheese

In a large soup pot, heat olive oil over medium heat. Add onion, garlic, basil, and salt and pepper and sauté till onion is translucent, about 4 to 5 minutes. Add canned tomatoes, 2½ cups broth, and sugar. Cover and simmer on low for 20 minutes.

In a blender, blend tofu and 1½ cups vegetable broth until smooth. Add to soup pot and stir in four of the diced tomatoes combined with ⅓ cup water. Garnish with remaining diced tomatoes and Cheddar cheese.

PER SERVING:
226 Calories; 11g Fat; 15g Protein; 21g Carbohydrate; 5g Dietary Fiber; 15mg Cholesterol; 643mg Sodium. Exchanges: 0 Grain (Starch); 1½ Lean Meat; 2½ Vegetable; 1½ Fat; ½ Other Carbohydrates.

SERVING SUGGESTIONS: Add a big spinach salad and corn muffins (make or buy extra and freeze to keep fresh for the Crock Cauliflower White Chili, page 199, for the last night of this week).

DO AHEAD TIP: Cook 6 cups of brown rice for the next two nights' meals.

CAJUN BEAN CONFETTI

Serves 6

3 tablespoons olive oil
2 large green bell peppers, seeded, deribbed, and diced
1 large red bell pepper, seeded, deribbed, and diced
1 large onion, chopped
3 garlic cloves, pressed
1½ teaspoons Cajun seasoning (more or less to taste)
3 cups cooked brown rice
1½ (14.5-ounce) cans low-sodium vegetable broth
½ (16-ounce) package frozen corn kernels
2 (14.5-ounce) cans red kidney beans, drained and rinsed
Salt and pepper to taste
6 drops hot pepper sauce (optional)

In a large skillet, heat olive oil over high heat. Add peppers, onion, garlic, and Cajun seasoning. Cook, stirring frequently, for about 3 minutes.

Add rice and stir to coat. Add broth and bring to a boil, covered. Stir in corn and beans. Cover and remove from heat. Let stand for 5 minutes. Season with salt and pepper and hot sauce, if desired.

PER SERVING:
492 Calories; 8g Fat; 18g Protein; 91g Carbohydrate; 12g Dietary Fiber; 0mg Cholesterol; 773mg Sodium. Exchanges: 5½ Grain (Starch); 1 Lean Meat; 1 Vegetable; 1½ Fat; 0 Other Carbohydrates.

SERVING SUGGESTIONS: Serve with coleslaw and corn muffins with honey butter.

DO AHEAD TIP: Cook brown rice for tomorrow night's meal if you haven't already done so.

BROCCOLI SAUTÉ

Serves 6

3 cups cooked brown rice
4 tablespoons olive oil
4 garlic cloves, pressed
4 medium tomatoes, diced
2 bunches broccoli florets, chopped
1½ teaspoons dried marjoram
Salt and pepper to taste
½ cup water
9 ounces feta cheese, crumbled (about 2 cups)

Cook rice according to package directions and keep warm. (If you used the do-ahead tip, warm your rice and set aside.)

In a large skillet, heat olive oil over medium-high heat. Add garlic and sauté for 2 minutes, being careful not to brown. Add tomatoes and cook, stirring for 2 more minutes. Add broccoli and marjoram, stirring well. Salt and pepper to taste. Pour in water, cover pan, and cook, stirring occasionally, for 5 minutes.

On each plate, make a bed of the hot rice, spoon broccoli mixture on top, sprinkle with feta cheese, and serve.

PER SERVING:
443 Calories; 20g Fat; 12g Protein; 55g Carbohydrate; 2g Dietary Fiber; 38mg Cholesterol; 487mg Sodium. Exchanges: 3 Grain (Starch); 1 Lean Meat; 1 Vegetable; 3½ Fat.

SERVING SUGGESTION: Serve with Carrot Slaw (see page 254).

STUFFED PEPPERS WITH COUSCOUS

Serves 6

1¼ cup whole wheat couscous

6 large green bell peppers, tops cut off, seeded, cored (reserve tops if
  desired)

1 medium zucchini, coarsely chopped

½ cup chopped cilantro

1 (16-ounce) can chickpeas, drained and rinsed

½ cup chopped green onion

¼ cup balsamic vinegar

2 teaspoons cumin

2 tablespoons olive oil

Salt and pepper to taste

¼ cup water

Preheat oven to 400 degrees F.

Prepare couscous according to package directions. Fluff with fork
and transfer to a large mixing bowl to cool.

Chop green bell pepper tops and add to the couscous, if desired.

Add zucchini, cilantro, chickpeas, green onions, vinegar, cumin,
olive oil, and salt and pepper to couscous. Toss well to combine, then
spoon into green bell peppers.

Place stuffed peppers into casserole dish with ¼ cup water. Bake for
about 30 minutes or until stuffing is warmed through and peppers are
tender.

PER SERVING:
525 Calories; 10g Fat; 22g Protein; 90g Carbohydrate; 18g Dietary Fiber; 0mg Cholesterol;
34mg Sodium. Exchanges: 5½ Grain (Starch); 1 Lean Meat; 1½ Vegetable; 0 Fruit; 1½ Fat.

SERVING SUGGESTIONS: Serve with baked sweet potatoes and some
steamed broccoli.

CROCK CAULIFLOWER WHITE CHILI

Serves 6

"The Crock Cauliflower White Chili is wonderfully spicy and exotically different, both creamy and hot—a surprise treat for nonvegetarian guests!"
—Nerys P.

1 tablespoon vegetable oil

2 medium onions, finely chopped

4 garlic cloves, pressed

½ tablespoon caraway seeds

1 tablespoon dried oregano

1 tablespoon chili powder

Salt and pepper to taste

1 (14.5-ounce) can white kidney beans, drained and rinsed

3 cups low-sodium vegetable broth

3 cups cauliflower florets

1 large green bell pepper, seeded, deribbed, and chopped

2 cups shredded Pepper Jack cheese

4 ounces cream cheese, cut into ½-inch cubes

1 (4.5-ounce) can chopped green chilies

In a skillet, heat oil over medium heat. Add onions and cook till softened, about 3 minutes. Add garlic, caraway seeds, oregano, chili powder, and salt and pepper and continue stirring and cooking for 1 minute.

In a slow cooker, combine onion mixture, beans, and broth. Cover and cook on low for 8 to 10 hours or on high for 4 to 5 hours.

Meanwhile, cook cauliflower florets in salted boiling water for 4 minutes; drain.

Stir cooked cauliflower into the slow cooker along with green bell pepper, cheese, cream cheese, and chilies. Cover and cook on high for 30 minutes or until the green bell peppers are softened and the cauliflower is cooked through.

424 Calories; 22g Fat; 27g Protein; 33g Carbohydrate; 10g Dietary Fiber; 60mg Cholesterol; 584mg Sodium. Exchanges: 1½ Grain (Starch); 2½ Lean Meat; 1½ Vegetable; 3½ Fat.

SERVING SUGGESTIONS: A big green salad and corn muffins would do the trick.

🍁 Week Two

DAY ONE: Mega-Garlic Pasta

DAY TWO: Tofu Tostadas

DAY THREE: Vegetable Couscous

DAY FOUR: Easy Cheesy Cauliflower Soup

DAY FIVE: Stuffed Spaghetti Squash

DAY SIX: "Sweet P" Combo

SHOPPING LIST

CONDIMENTS

Olive oil

Salsa, your favorite (3 cups)

**Salad dressing, your favorite (4 meals)

**Rice vinegar (1 meal)

**Mayonnaise (1 meal)

PRODUCE

1 (14–16-ounce) package firm tofu

3 pounds yellow onions (keep on hand)

3–4 garlic heads

2 medium green bell peppers

12 mushrooms

12 large carrots; **additional (1 meal)

2 medium red potatoes

2 parsnips

2 medium zucchini

2 medium yellow summer squash

1 large head cauliflower

3 medium spaghetti squash

3 sweet potatoes

Lettuce (optional garnish)

Avocados (optional garnish)

1 bunch basil

1 bunch cilantro

**Lettuce, not iceberg (3 meals)

**Spinach (1 meal)

**Salad toppings (4 meals)

**Broccoli slaw (2 meals)

**Broccoli (1 meal)

CANNED GOODS

5 (14.5-ounce) cans low-sodium vegetable broth

1 (14.5-ounce) can diced tomatoes

1 (8-ounce) can tomato juice

3 (15-ounce) cans chickpeas

2 (4.5-ounce) cans chopped green chilies

2 (14-ounce) cans crushed pineapple in juice

SPICES AND DRIED HERBS

Tarragon

Oregano

Dillweed

Thyme

Cumin

Caraway seeds

Curry powder

Red pepper flakes

DAIRY/DAIRY CASE

Butter

Sour cream (optional garnish)

Grated Parmesan cheese (¾ cup)

Shredded Cheddar cheese (3 cups); additional (optional garnish)

Grated romano cheese (½ cup)

DRY GOODS

Brown sugar

Linguine pasta (12 ounces)

Long-grain white rice (½ cup)

Couscous (1¼ cups)

Lentils (3 cups)

Bread crumbs (1 cup)

Golden raisins (⅓ cup)

BREADS/BAKERY

**Whole-grain rolls (2 meals)

6 corn tortillas

FROZEN FOODS

1 (16-ounce) package frozen corn kernels

MEGA-GARLIC PASTA

Serves 6

12 ounces linguine
4 tablespoons olive oil
12 garlic cloves, pressed
3 teaspoons red pepper flakes
Salt and pepper to taste
1 cup chopped fresh basil leaves
¾ cup grated Parmesan cheese

Cook pasta according to package directions until al dente. Drain and keep warm.

Meanwhile, in a small skillet, heat 2 tablespoons of oil over medium-low heat. Add garlic, pepper flakes, and salt and pepper and sauté till garlic is tender.

Toss pasta with remaining 2 tablespoons oil, basil, and garlic mixture. Garnish with Parmesan cheese.

PER SERVING:
345 Calories; 13g Fat; 12g Protein; 45g Carbohydrate; 2g Dietary Fiber; 8mg Cholesterol; 191mg Sodium. Exchanges: 3 Grain (Starch); ½ Lean Meat; ½ Vegetable; 2 Fat.

SERVING SUGGESTIONS: Serve pasta with a big green salad with lots of shredded veggies, like carrots, broccoli, and cabbage (you can buy cabbage and broccoli slaw already prepared).

TOFU TOSTADAS

2 tablespoons olive oil

1 large onion, chopped

2 medium green bell peppers, seeded, deribbed, and chopped

1 (14–16-ounce) package tofu, drained and cubed

3 cups salsa

1½ (4.5-ounce) cans chopped green chiles

1½ teaspoons cumin

1 teaspoon dried oregano

1½ cups frozen corn kernels

6 tablespoons minced cilantro

6 corn tortillas

OPTIONAL GARNISHES

Shredded Cheddar cheese

Light sour cream

Lettuce

Guacamole

In a large skillet, heat oil over medium-high heat. Add onion and green bell peppers, and sauté for 2 to 3 minutes, till veggies are slightly softened. Add tofu, tossing to coat. Stir in salsa, green chilis, cumin, oregano, and corn and cook for 3 minutes, stirring frequently, till heated through. Stir in cilantro.

Heat a nonstick skillet over medium heat and toast tortillas, one at a time, for 2 to 3 minutes on each side. Evenly divide tofu mixture onto the tortillas and serve.

PER SERVING:
259 Calories; 9g Fat; 12g Protein; 38g Carbohydrate; 6g Dietary Fiber; 0mg Cholesterol; 617mg Sodium. Exchanges: 1½ Grain (Starch); 1½ Lean Meat; 2½ Vegetable; 1½ Fat.

SERVING SUGGESTIONS: Serve with the optional garnishes and a big green salad.

VEGETABLE COUSCOUS

Serves 6

3 tablespoons olive oil
2½ medium onions, thinly sliced
3 large carrots, sliced ½-inch thick
2 medium red potatoes, cut into ½-inch cubes
4 garlic cloves, pressed
5 cups low-sodium vegetable broth
1 (14.5-ounce) can diced tomatoes
1 teaspoon dried tarragon
Salt and pepper to taste
2 parsnips, peeled and sliced ½-inch thick
2 medium zucchini, sliced ½-inch thick
2 medium yellow summer squash, sliced ½-inch thick
2½ cups cooked chickpeas
⅓ cup golden raisins
1¼ cups couscous

In a large soup pot, heat 2 tablespoons of oil over medium heat. Add onions and sauté for about 5 minutes, until golden. Add carrots, potatoes, and garlic, and cook for 2 minutes, stirring frequently. Stir in broth, tomatoes, tarragon, and salt and pepper. Bring to a boil; lower heat and simmer, covered, for 5 minutes. Add parsnips and simmer, covered, for another 3 minutes. Add zucchini, squash, and chickpeas and simmer, covered, for 8 minutes or until the veggies are just tender.

With a glass measuring cup, transfer 1½ cups of cooking liquid from the soup pot to a small saucepan. Stir in raisins and remaining 1 tablespoon of oil; bring liquid to a boil and stir in couscous. Remove from heat and let stand, covered, for 10 minutes. Serve the veggies over the couscous.

PER SERVING:
520 Calories; 9g Fat; 24g Protein; 89g Carbohydrate; 16g Dietary Fiber; 0mg Cholesterol; 569mg Sodium. Exchanges: 4 Grain (Starch); 1½ Lean Meat; 3 Vegetable; ½ Fruit; 1½ Fat.

SERVING SUGGESTION: Serve with steamed broccoli.

EASY CHEESY CAULIFLOWER SOUP

Serves 6

2 tablespoons butter
1 medium onion, chopped
3 garlic cloves, pressed
1 teaspoon dillweed
½ teaspoon caraway seeds
2 cups water
2 cups low-sodium vegetable broth
½ cup long-grain white rice
5 cups cauliflower florets (about 1 large head)
Salt and pepper to taste
¾ cup tomato juice
3 cups shredded Cheddar cheese

In a large, heavy saucepan, melt butter over medium heat. Add onion and garlic, and sauté for 3 minutes. Stir in dillweed, caraway seeds, water, broth, rice, and 3 cups of cauliflower florets and bring to a boil. Lower heat and simmer gently, covered, for 20 minutes. Stir in salt and pepper.

Meanwhile, steam remaining 2 cups of cauliflower; drain and keep warm.

Drain rice and cauliflower mixture over a bowl, reserving liquid. Add tomato juice to mixture and purée in a blender or food processor; transfer to large soup pot.

Add steamed cauliflower, reserved liquid, and 2 cups of Cheddar cheese to purée. Heat gently and serve topped with extra cheese.

PER SERVING:
371 Calories; 23g Fat; 21g Protein; 22g Carbohydrate; 4g Dietary Fiber; 70mg Cholesterol; 702mg Sodium. Exchanges: 1 Grain (Starch); 2½ Lean Meat; 1½ Vegetable; 3½ Fat.

SERVING SUGGESTIONS: Serve with a big green salad and whole-grain rolls.

DO AHEAD TIP: Cook lentils for tomorrow night's meal.

Squash the Rumors

Have you noticed the proliferation of winter squashes this time of year? Those lovely hard gourds that we love to display on our Thanksgiving sideboards are actually quite delicious—once you know how to crack their cases, that is. In the original *Saving Dinner* book, I gave instructions for dealing with these hardened squashes.

I get e-mails all the time from intrepid cooks, wondering what the heck to do with the marvelous butternut squash I suggested for the week's Menu-Mailer. It can be intimidating until you've learned the secret of unlocking the winter squash. The cookbooks I've read all tell you the same thing when preparing winter squash: "use a sharp knife and cut the squash in half." Well, if you're buying quality squash (look for firm squash—no soft spots allowed), that thing is harder to break into than a childproof top on a bottle of aspirin. Give me a break! Here's the way I do squash:

First off, wash it and stab it a few times. (No Norman Bates imitations; go easy.)

Next, put your stabbed darling into a preheated (350 degree F. oven) for 10 to 15 minutes, depending on the size. Throw it right on the rack—no pan necessary.

When the time is up, pull the squash from the oven and set it aside. Now futz with your salad or whatever else you need to do to get dinner ready. When the squash is cool enough to handle, proceed with the peeling and seeding and cubing of your gourd. Place in a baking dish and bake till tender. You can add a little orange juice, water, broth—anything to give it a little moisture. Top with a little bit of herbs, too. If you used orange juice, try some cinnamon or nutmeg. If you added water, go with just about anything. If you used broth, a little sage or thyme works well. When the squash is tender, it's done. Use a fork to smush it into a purée, add a little honey or maple syrup if you cooked it with cinnamon and nutmeg, and enjoy—you've earned that delicious squash!

STUFFED SPAGHETTI SQUASH

Serves 6

3 cups lentils, cooked

3 medium spaghetti squash, halved and cored

3 tablespoons olive oil

2 large onions, chopped

3 garlic cloves, pressed

12 mushrooms, cleaned and chopped

Salt and pepper to taste

1 teaspoon dried thyme

1 cup bread crumbs

½ cup grated Romano cheese

Preheat oven to 350 degrees F.

Cook lentils according to package directions, if you have not already.

Cut squash lengthwise in half and scoop out seeds. Be sure to leave meat! Lay squash face up on a cookie sheet, cutting off a piece of the squash bottom if it won't lie flat.

In a skillet, heat oil over medium-high heat. Sauté onions, garlic, and mushrooms till onions are translucent, about 4 to 5 minutes. Add salt and pepper, thyme, lentils, and bread crumbs and cook for 3 more minutes.

Spoon the stuffing mixture into each squash half. Sprinkle with cheese and bake for 30 minutes, or till the squash is easily pierced with a fork.

PER SERVING:
533 Calories; 12g Fat; 34g Protein; 77g Carbohydrate; 31g Dietary Fiber; 10mg Cholesterol; 288mg Sodium. Exchanges: 4½ Grain (Starch); 2½ Lean Meat; 1½ Vegetable; 2 Fat.

SERVING SUGGESTION: Serve with a big spinach salad.

"SWEET P" COMBO

Serves 6

3 sweet potatoes, peeled and cut into ½-inch cubes

9 carrots, peeled and thinly sliced

1½ (14-ounce) cans crushed pineapple in juice, drained and juice
    reserved

2 tablespoons brown sugar, packed

1 (15-ounce) can chickpeas, drained and rinsed

2 garlic cloves, pressed

¾ cup low-sodium vegetable broth

½ teaspoon curry powder (more or less to taste)

Salt and pepper to taste

In a greased slow cooker, combine sweet potatoes, carrots, and pineapple. In a small bowl, combine the brown sugar and ½ cup reserved pineapple juice; add to slow cooker and stir till blended.

In a food processor or blender, process chickpeas, garlic, vegetable broth, and curry powder till well blended but chickpeas still a bit chunky.

Season with salt and pepper. Spread mixture evenly over sweet potato mixture. Cover and cook on low for 6 to 8 hours, or till veggies are tender.

PER SERVING:
289 Calories; 1g Fat; 8g Protein; 65g Carbohydrate; 9g Dietary Fiber; 0mg Cholesterol; 325mg Sodium. Exchanges: 2 Grain (Starch); 0 Lean Meat; 2 Vegetable; 1 Fruit; 0 Fat; 0 Other Carbohydrates.

SERVING SUGGESTIONS: Serve with Broccoli Slaw (see page 254) and whole-grain rolls.

Week Three

DAY ONE: Pears and Pecans Noodle Salad

DAY TWO: Seasoned Veggies and Tofu

DAY THREE: Fiesta Bean Casserole

DAY FOUR: Lentil and Leek Risotto

DAY FIVE: Carrot-Mushroom Casserole

DAY SIX: Greek Cannellini

SHOPPING LIST

CONDIMENTS

Olive oil

Vegetable oil

Balsamic vinegar

Salsa, your favorite (1 cup)

Kalamata olives, pitted (20)

1 (9-ounce) jar roasted red peppers

**Salad dressing, your favorite (2 meals)

PRODUCE

2 (14–16-ounce) packages firm tofu

3 pounds yellow onions (keep on hand)

1 small red onion

6 leeks

3 garlic heads; **additional (1 meal)

3 green bell peppers

2 red bell peppers

1 bunch celery

1 (16-ounce) carton mushrooms

1 pound carrots

12 ounces spinach leaves

2 heads cauliflower

1 bunch parsley

3 pears

1–2 oranges (for ⅓ cup juice)

1 lemon (for 1 tablespoon juice)

Avocado (1 meal)

**Broccoli (1 meal)

**Baby carrots (1 meal)

**Grape tomatoes (1 meal)

**Kale (1 meal)

**Baby greens (1 meal)

**Lettuce, not iceberg (1 meal)

**Spinach (1 meal)

**Salad toppings (3 meals)

CANNED GOODS

4 (14.5-ounce) cans low-sodium vegetable broth

3 (28-ounce) cans diced tomatoes

2 (14-ounce) cans red kidney beans

2 (15-ounce) cans cannellini beans (white beans)

1 (14-ounce) can corn

SPICES AND DRIED HERBS

Rosemary

Parsley

Oregano

Basil

Thyme

Red pepper flakes

Italian seasoning

DAIRY/DAIRY CASE

Eggs (2)

Blue cheese crumbles (½ cup)

Shredded Cheddar cheese (5 cups)

Sour cream

**Butter (2 meals)

DRY GOODS

Egg noodles (1 pound)

Brown rice (2 cups); **additional (3 meals)

Lentils (1½ cups)

Bread crumbs (2 cups)

Pecan pieces (¼ cup)

BREADS/BAKERY

12 corn tortillas

**Whole-grain rolls (1 meal)

**Whole-grain bread (1 meal)

FROZEN FOODS

1 (20-ounce) package baby lima beans

PEARS AND PECANS NOODLE SALAD

Serves 6

9 ounces egg noodles

⅓ cup orange juice

3 tablespoons balsamic vinegar

1 tablespoons lemon juice

2 garlic cloves, pressed

1 tablespoon olive oil

Salt and pepper to taste

12 ounces spinach leaves, cut into 1-inch crosswise strips

3 pears, cored and sliced (not peeled)

½ cup crumbled blue cheese

¼ cup pecan pieces

1 small red onion, thinly sliced

Prepare noodles according to package directions. Drain and place in a large bowl.

In a small bowl, whisk together orange juice, balsamic vinegar, lemon juice, garlic, oil, and salt and pepper for dressing.

In a large skillet, heat 2 tablespoons of dressing over medium heat. Sauté spinach in two to three batches, until slightly wilted, about 1 to 2 minutes max.

In a large bowl, combine cooked noodles, pears, half the cheese, half the pecans, wilted spinach, and red onion. Add remaining dressing and toss gently to combine. Sprinkle remaining cheese and pecans over top.

PER SERVING:
299 Calories; 8g Fat; 10g Protein; 49g Carbohydrate; 5g Dietary Fiber; 48mg Cholesterol; 174mg Sodium. Exchanges: 2 Grain (Starch); ½ Lean Meat; ½ Vegetable; 1 Fruit; 1 Fat.

SERVING SUGGESTIONS: Serve with baby carrots and grape tomatoes on the side.

SEASONED VEGGIES AND TOFU

Serves 6

6 tablespoons olive oil
1½ (14–16-ounce) packages firm tofu, drained and cubed
9 garlic cloves, pressed
¼ teaspoon red pepper flakes
1½ (28-ounce) cans diced tomatoes
1½ tablespoons Italian seasoning
Salt and pepper to taste
6 cups cauliflower florets
3 cups frozen baby lima beans, thawed

In a large soup pot, heat 4 tablespoons of olive oil over medium-high heat. Add tofu and cook till golden brown, about 5 minutes. Remove to platter.

Pour in remaining 2 tablespoons oil and reduce heat to medium. Sauté garlic and red pepper flakes for about 2 minutes. Immediately add tomatoes, Italian seasoning, salt, and pepper and bring to a boil. Cook 3 minutes and then add the cauliflower and lima beans. Cook, stirring occasionally, for about 15 minutes till cauliflower is tender. Don't let it get mushy!

Return the tofu to the pot and cook until heated through, about 3 minutes.

PER SERVING:
386 Calories; 19g Fat; 19g Protein; 40g Carbohydrate; 9g Dietary Fiber; 0mg Cholesterol; 376mg Sodium. Exchanges: 1½ Grain (Starch); 2½ Lean Meat; 3 Vegetable; 3½ Fat.

SERVING SUGGESTIONS: Serve with brown rice (make extra for tomorrow night's Serving Suggestions) and steamed broccoli.

FIESTA BEAN CASSEROLE

1 large onion, chopped
2 green bell peppers, seeded, deribbed, and chopped
1 cup salsa
2 garlic cloves, pressed
1 (28-ounce) can diced tomatoes
2 (14-ounce) cans red kidney beans, drained
1 (14-ounce) can corn, drained
12 corn tortillas
3 cups shredded Cheddar cheese
1 cup sour cream
1 avocado, sliced

Lightly grease a 9 × 13-inch baking dish. Preheat oven to 350 degrees F.

In a large skillet, combine onion, bell peppers, salsa, and garlic and cook for about 5 minutes. Add tomatoes, beans, and corn and heat through.

Place one-third of the veggie mixture in the greased baking dish, then put six tortillas on top. Sprinkle with 1 cup of cheese. Repeat layers, ending with the last third of the veggie mixture on top.

Cook for 25 minutes; add any remaining cheese and cook for 5 more minutes. Top casserole with sour cream and sliced avocado.

PER SERVING:
550 Calories; 21g Fat; 27g Protein; 68g Carbohydrate; 15g Dietary Fiber; 59mg Cholesterol; 1537mg Sodium. Exchanges: 3½ Grain (Starch); 2½ Lean Meat; 2½ Vegetable; 2½ Fat.

SERVING SUGGESTIONS: Serve with brown rice and a big green salad.

LENTIL AND LEEK RISOTTO

Serves 6

1½ cups lentils
2 tablespoons olive oil
3 cups cleaned and chopped leeks
2 garlic cloves
1 green bell pepper, seeded, deribbed, and finely chopped
4½ cups low-sodium vegetable broth
2 cups brown rice
Salt and pepper to taste
1½ teaspoons dried thyme
½ cup chopped fresh parsley
½ cup finely chopped carrots

Cook lentils according to package directions, if you haven't already done so.

In a large soup pot, heat oil over medium heat. Sauté leeks, garlic, and green bell pepper till soft, about 4 to 5 minutes. Add broth, rice, salt and pepper, and thyme. Reduce heat and simmer, covered, for about 40 minutes or until rice is done. Uncover, stir in lentils, and heat through. Garnish with parsley and carrots.

PER SERVING:
488 Calories; 9g Fat; 15g Protein; 87g Carbohydrate; 9g Dietary Fiber; 2mg Cholesterol; 1239mg Sodium. Exchanges: 5 Grain (Starch); ½ Lean Meat; 1½ Vegetable; 2 Fat.

SERVING SUGGESTIONS: Serve with a baby greens salad and whole-grain rolls and butter.

CARROT-MUSHROOM CASSEROLE

Serves 6

1 tablespoon olive oil
2 medium onions, chopped
1 (16-ounce) carton mushrooms, cleaned and chopped
Salt and pepper to taste
1 teaspoon dried thyme
1 teaspoon dried rosemary
1 teaspoon dried parsley
4 garlic cloves, pressed
6 cups grated carrots
2 cups bread crumbs
2 cups shredded Cheddar cheese
2 eggs, beaten

Lightly oil a 9 × 13-inch baking dish. Preheat oven to 350 degrees F.

In a large skillet, heat oil over medium heat. Sauté onions for about 5 minutes. Add mushrooms, salt and pepper, thyme, rosemary, parsley, and garlic; continue to cook for about 10 more minutes.

In a large bowl, combine carrots, bread crumbs, 1 cup of cheese, and eggs. Add sautéed mixture and mix well. Spread into prepared pan. Cover with foil and bake for 30 minutes. Uncover and bake 15 more minutes, sprinkling with remaining cheese the last 5 minutes.

PER SERVING:
437 Calories; 19g Fat; 20g Protein; 49g Carbohydrate; 7g Dietary Fiber; 110mg Cholesterol; 618mg Sodium. Exchanges: 1½ Grain (Starch); 1½ Lean Meat; 4 Vegetable; 2½ Fat.

SERVING SUGGESTIONS: Serve with a spinach salad and whole-grain bread and butter.

GREEK CANNELLINI

Serves 6

1 tablespoon vegetable oil
2 onions, finely chopped
4 celery stalks, chopped
4 garlic cloves, pressed
1 teaspoon dried oregano
1 teaspoon dried basil
Salt and pepper to taste
1½ (15-ounce) cans cannellini beans, drained
2½ cups low-sodium vegetable broth
1 (9-ounce) jar roasted red peppers, drained and cut into strips
20 Kalamata olives, thinly sliced (get the pitted ones to make it easier)

In a skillet, heat oil over medium heat. Add onions and celery, and cook, stirring, till veggies are softened, 5 to 7 minutes. Add garlic, oregano, basil, and salt and pepper and stir for another minute.

Transfer mixture to slow cooker. Add beans and broth. Cover and cook on low for 8 to 10 hours or on high for 4 to 5 hours. Stir in roasted peppers and olives before serving.

PER SERVING:
539 Calories; 5g Fat; 37g Protein; 90g Carbohydrate; 24g Dietary Fiber; 0mg Cholesterol; 391mg Sodium. Exchanges: 5½ Grain (Starch); 2½ Lean Meat; 1 Vegetable; 0 Fruit; 1 Fat.

SERVING SUGGESTIONS: Serve with brown rice and Braised Kale (see page 259).

Week Four

DAY ONE: Peppery Fusilli

DAY TWO: Delectable Chili

DAY THREE: Tofu Manicotti

DAY FOUR: Scalloped Kale and Potatoes

DAY FIVE: Barley Mushroom Casserole

DAY SIX: Cheesy Corn Loaf

SHOPPING LIST

CONDIMENTS

Olive oil

Bragg Liquid Aminos (look in the health food
    section/store) or low-sodium soy sauce

**Salad dressing, your favorite (3 meals)

**Rice vinegar (2 meals)

**Mayonnaise (2 meals)

**Honey (1 meal)

PRODUCE

1 (14–16-ounce) package soft tofu

3 pounds yellow onions (keep on hand)

1 bunch green onions

3 leeks

3 garlic heads

2 large green bell peppers

2 red bell peppers (1 large, 1 small)

13 mushrooms

2 pounds kale

10 medium russet potatoes

1 bunch basil

1 bunch parsley

**Lettuce, not iceberg (1 meal)

**Romaine lettuce (1 meal)

**Spinach (1 meal)

**Salad toppings (3 meals)

**Coleslaw mix (1 meal)

**Broccoli slaw mix (1 meal)

**Baby carrots (1 meal)

**Sweet potatoes (1 meal)

**Sugar snap peas (1 meal)

CANNED GOODS

4 (14.5-ounce) cans low-sodium vegetable broth

2 (14-ounce) cans red kidney beans

1 (15-ounce) can chickpeas

1 (32-ounce) can tomato juice

SPICES AND DRIED HERBS

Marjoram

Thyme

Sage

Bay leaf

Cumin

Garlic powder

Chili powder

Red pepper flakes

**Cinnamon

DAIRY/DAIRY CASE

Butter

Eggs (4)

Egg whites (2)

Milk (2%)

Grated Parmesan cheese (⅔ cup)

Shredded Cheddar cheese (¾ cup)

Shredded Monterey Jack cheese (3 cups)

Ricotta cheese (8 ounces)

DRY GOODS

Flour

Fusilli pasta (24 ounces)

12 manicotti shells

Pearl barley (1 cup)

½ ounce dried mushrooms

BREADS/BAKERY

**Garlic bread (2 meals)

**Cornbread (1 meal)

FROZEN FOODS

1 (20-ounce) package frozen corn kernels

PEPPERY FUSILLI

Serves 6

1½ pounds fusilli
3½ tablespoons olive oil
4 medium yellow onions, thinly sliced
4 garlic cloves, pressed
2 large green bell peppers, seeded, deribbed, and thinly sliced
1 large red bell pepper, seeded, deribbed, and thinly sliced
3 tablespoons minced fresh basil
1½ teaspoons red pepper flakes
3 tablespoons flour
3 cups low-sodium vegetable broth
Salt and pepper to taste

Cook pasta according to package directions until al dente. Drain and transfer to a warm serving bowl.

In a skillet, heat 2 tablespoons oil over medium-high heat. Add onions and sauté for 5 minutes. Reduce heat and add garlic, bell peppers, basil, and red pepper flakes; cook, stirring occasionally, for 15 minutes.

In a small saucepan, heat remaining 1½ tablespoons oil over medium heat. Stir in flour and cook for 30 seconds. Gradually add broth and bring to a boil. Cook, stirring constantly, for 5 minutes or until smooth and thickened. Season with salt and pepper.

Stir sauce into the cooked veggies and toss the mixture with the warm pasta.

PER SERVING:
577 Calories; 10g Fat; 22g Protein; 100g Carbohydrate; 7g Dietary Fiber; 0mg Cholesterol; 271mg Sodium. Exchanges: 6 Grain (Starch); ½ Lean Meat; 2 Vegetable; 2 Fat.

SERVING SUGGESTIONS: Serve with a big green salad and garlic bread.

DELECTABLE CHILI

Serves 6

1 tablespoon olive oil
1 medium onion, chopped
2 garlic cloves, pressed
2 (14-ounce) cans red kidney beans
1 (15-ounce) can chickpeas
4 cups tomato juice
2 tablespoons chili powder
1 tablespoon cumin
Salt and pepper to taste

In a large pot, heat oil over medium-high heat and cook onion and garlic till onion is translucent, about 3 to 4 minutes. Add remaining ingredients and stir together. Simmer on medium-low heat for 40 to 60 minutes, stirring occasionally.

PER SERVING:
396 Calories; 6g Fat; 22g Protein; 68g Carbohydrate; 18g Dietary Fiber; 0mg Cholesterol; 630mg Sodium. Exchanges: 4 Grain (Starch); 1½ Lean Meat; 1½ Vegetable; 1 Fat.

SERVING SUGGESTIONS: Serve with coleslaw and cornbread with honey butter.

DO AHEAD TIP: Prepare manicotti for tomorrow night's meal. Then all you'll need to do is slip it into the oven and dinner will be almost ready by the time you get your table set.

TOFU MANICOTTI

12 manicotti shells
3 tablespoons olive oil
¾ cup chopped onion
¾ cup cleaned and chopped mushrooms
1½ tablespoons chopped fresh parsley
1½ teaspoons dried thyme
½ teaspoon dried sage
1 (14–16-ounce) package soft tofu, drained
2 egg whites, slightly beaten
3 tablespoons grated Parmesan cheese
1¾ cups low-fat milk
3 tablespoons flour
⅛ teaspoon garlic powder
Salt and pepper to taste
¾ cup shredded Cheddar cheese

Preheat oven to 350 degrees F.

Cook shells according to package directions until al dente. Rinse in cold water and drain.

In a skillet, heat oil over medium heat. Add onion and mushrooms and cook till tender, about 4 to 5 minutes. Stir in parsley, thyme, and sage; cool slightly.

In a blender or food processor, place tofu, egg whites, and Parmesan cheese and blend until smooth. Remove tofu mixture from blender to bowl, stir in onion and mushrooms, and stuff each manicotti shell with about ¼ cup tofu mixture. Arrange stuffed shells in a 9 × 13-inch baking dish.

In a medium saucepan, combine milk, flour, garlic powder, and salt and pepper. Cook over medium-low heat till thick and bubbly. Stir often. Pour sauce over stuffed shells.

Bake covered, for about 20 minutes. Sprinkle with Cheddar cheese. Bake, uncovered, for another 5 minutes or till cheese melts.

PER SERVING:
376 Calories; 18g Fat; 19g Protein; 36g Carbohydrate; 2g Dietary Fiber; 22mg Cholesterol; 197mg Sodium. Exchanges: 2 Grain (Starch); 1½ Lean Meat; ½ Vegetable; ½ Non-Fat Milk; 2½ Fat; 0 Other Carbohydrates.

SERVING SUGGESTIONS: Serve with a simple romaine salad and garlic bread.

SCALLOPED KALE AND POTATOES

2 pounds kale
½ cup water
10 medium potatoes, peeled and thinly sliced
4 garlic cloves, pressed
3 cups grated Monterey Jack cheese
12 tablespoons butter, cut into bits
Salt and pepper to taste
2½ cups low-fat milk

Generously grease a large, shallow baking dish. Preheat oven to 425 degrees F.

Thoroughly rinse kale and shake off excess water; remove tough stems. In a medium saucepan, combine kale with water. Cook about 7 minutes, till the kale just wilts. Drain and cool. Squeeze out the remaining water with your hands. Coarsely chop the kale and set aside.

Place half the potato slices in the baking dish. Next layer with all the kale, then sprinkle on the garlic and half the cheese, butter, and salt and pepper. Top with remaining potato slices, cheese, butter, and salt and pepper.

Pour the milk over the whole dish and gently shake to make sure it goes through all the layers. Bake for 50 minutes or till potatoes are soft and browned.

PER SERVING:
689 Calories; 42g Fat; 27g Protein; 58g Carbohydrate; 6g Dietary Fiber; 114mg Cholesterol; 667mg Sodium. Exchanges: 2½ Grain (Starch); 2 Lean Meat; 3 Vegetable; ½ Non-Fat Milk; 7 Fat.

SERVING SUGGESTIONS: Serve with Broccoli Slaw (see page 254) and a bowl of baby carrots.

Bragg On

Bragg Liquid Aminos is a great alternative to soy sauce, and for some advocates, it's the only way to "do" soy sauce.

What is it anyway? It's made from soy, as is soy sauce, but the process is cleaner (no fermentation) and there are no salt or preservatives added—the process makes its own salty taste from the natural-occurring salt in the soybeans. The flavor is very much like soy sauce (not quite so strong), and the bonus is that it contains amino acids—the building blocks for the body.

The fact that this is a raw product, non-genetically modified, and kosher are big factors for some people in deciding to use this for regular soy sauce. For me, I go with flavor and I like the mild flavor of Bragg sometimes and the punch of soy sauce at other times. It's just one of those things you'll want to try yourself.

BARLEY MUSHROOM CASSEROLE

Serves 6

½ ounce dried mushrooms
1 cup boiling water
4 teaspoons butter
1 cup pearl barley
1 medium onion, chopped
8 fresh mushrooms, cleaned and sliced
3 garlic cloves, pressed
2 cups low-sodium vegetable broth
Salt and pepper to taste
1 tablespoon Bragg Liquid Aminos or low-sodium soy sauce
1 bay leaf
¼ cup chopped green onions

Grease a medium casserole dish. Preheat oven to 350 degrees F.

In a small heatproof bowl, soak dried mushrooms in boiling water for 10 minutes. Drain in a colander lined with paper towels over a bowl and save the liquid. Chop the mushrooms.

In a large skillet, melt 2 teaspoons butter over medium heat. Add barley and sauté for 1 minute or till lightly browned. Transfer barley to a small bowl.

In the same skillet, melt remaining 2 teaspoons butter. Add onion and sauté for a couple of minutes, till translucent. Add fresh mushrooms and garlic; sauté for 3 minutes more. Return barley to the skillet and add soaked mushrooms and their liquid, the broth, salt and pepper, the Bragg, and the bay leaf; bring to a boil.

Transfer barley mixture to casserole dish and bake, covered, for 1 to 1¼ hours or till barley is tender. Before serving, remove the bay leaf and stir in the green onions.

PER SERVING:
218 Calories; 4g Fat; 7g Protein; 40g Carbohydrate; 7g Dietary Fiber; 8mg Cholesterol; 674mg Sodium. Exchanges: 2½ Grain (Starch); 1 Vegetable; 1 Fat.

SERVING SUGGESTION: Serve with a big spinach salad.

CHEESY CORN LOAF

Serves 6

8 ounces ricotta cheese
½ cup freshly grated Parmesan cheese
4 eggs, beaten
2 cups frozen corn kernels, thawed
2 tablespoons olive oil
3 leeks, white part only with a tad of green; cleaned and thinly sliced
4 garlic cloves, pressed
¼ cup seeded, deribbed, and diced red bell pepper
Salt and pepper to taste
½ teaspoon dried marjoram
1 tablespoon flour
1 cup low-sodium vegetable broth
Boiling water

Lightly grease an 8 × 5-inch loaf pan.

In a bowl, combine ricotta and Parmesan cheeses with eggs. Beat with a wooden spoon till smooth. Fold in corn. Set aside.

In a skillet, heat oil over medium heat. Add leeks and cook, stirring, about 4 minutes. Add garlic, bell pepper, salt and pepper, and marjoram and cook, stirring for 1 minute. Sprinkle flour over top of the veggies. Add vegetable broth and cook, stirring, until thickened. Fold into cheese mixture. Spoon mixture into prepared loaf pan.

Cover with foil. Place pan in slow cooker and pour in enough boiling water to reach 1 inch up the sides of the pan. Cover and cook on high for 4 hours, until set.

Carefully remove pan from slow cooker when ready to serve.

PER SERVING:
278 Calories; 15g Fat; 16g Protein; 22g Carbohydrate; 3g Dietary Fiber; 166mg Cholesterol; 300mg Sodium. Exchanges: 1 Grain (Starch); 1½ Lean Meat; 1½ Vegetable; 2 Fat.

SERVING SUGGESTIONS: Serve with Sweet Potato Fries (see page 258) and sautéed sugar snap peas.

❧ Week Five

"I am not a vegetarian but have always been intrigued by the idea. I was under the impression that vegetarian meals are boring and bland. This week's worth of menus has been poetry for my taste buds. I was aware of different textures and subtle flavors. I was amazed at the number of vegetables I ate and tried this week and I can honestly say that I felt great. I seemed to have more energy! Thank you!"   —Monika R.

DAY ONE: Vegetable Pasta Bake

DAY TWO: Tofu Surprise

DAY THREE: Late-Autumn Medley

DAY FOUR: Eggplant Bake

DAY FIVE: Leek and Potato Crustless Quiche

DAY SIX: Cheesy Rice Casserole

SHOPPING LIST

CONDIMENTS

Olive oil

Vinegar (if using white grape juice)

White wine (if not using white grape juice)

White grape juice (if not using white wine)

Soy sauce, low-sodium if available

1 (4-ounce) jar pimientos

1 (6.5-ounce) jar sun-dried tomatoes in oil

**Salad dressing, your favorite (3 meals)

**Vinaigrette dressing (1 meal)

**Rice vinegar (1 meal)

**Mayonnaise (1 meal)

PRODUCE

2 (14–16-ounce) packages firm tofu

5 pounds yellow onions (keep on hand)

3 medium leeks

2 garlic heads

1 bunch celery

3 (10-ounce) cartons mushrooms

1 large yellow summer squash

1 large acorn squash

1 small zucchini

2 large russet potatoes

1 large sweet potato

2 large eggplants

6 carrots

1 (10-ounce) bundle watercress (or use spinach)

8 ounces spinach (additional 10 ounces if not using watercress); **additional (1 meal)

1 knob ginger root

1 bunch basil

1 bunch cilantro

2 lemons (for ¼ cup juice)

2–3 limes (for 3 tablespoons juice)

**Baby greens (1 meal)

**Lettuce, not iceberg (2 meals)

**Salad toppings (3 meals)

**Broccoli slaw mix (1 meal)

**Baby carrots (1 meal)

**Tomatoes (1 meal)

CANNED GOODS

2 (14.5-ounce) cans low-sodium vegetable broth

2 (28-ounce) cans diced tomatoes

1 (14.5-ounce) can diced tomatoes

1 (15-ounce) can black beans

1 (28-ounce) jar spaghetti sauce, your favorite

SPICES AND DRIED HERBS

Marjoram

Cumin

Red pepper flakes

DAIRY/DAIRY CASE

Eggs (2)

Egg whites, large (1)

Skim milk

Mozzarella cheese (8 ounces)

Grated Parmesan cheese (3 tablespoons)

Shredded Cheddar cheese (2 cups)

Small-curd cottage cheese (½ cup)

**Feta cheese crumbles (1 meal)

**Butter

**Blend of shredded Cheddar/Jack cheese (1 meal)

DRY GOODS

Mostaccioli pasta (3 cups)

Long-grain brown rice (5 cups)

Unsalted dry-roasted peanuts (½ cup)

Currants (½ cup)

BREADS/BAKERY

**Whole wheat tortillas (1 meal)

**Whole-grain rolls (3 meals)

FROZEN FOODS

1 (20-ounce) package frozen corn kernels

VEGETABLE PASTA BAKE

Serves 6

3 cups mostaccioli pasta
2 tablespoons olive oil
1 large onion, chopped
2 garlic cloves, pressed
1 (28-ounce) jar spaghetti sauce
1 tablespoon fresh basil
8 ounces shredded mozzarella cheese
2 cups cleaned and sliced mushrooms
1 cup sliced yellow summer squash
1 cup sliced zucchini
2 cups thinly sliced carrots

Preheat oven to 375 degrees F.

Cook the pasta according to package directions until al dente. Drain and keep warm.

In a skillet, heat oil over medium heat. Add onion and garlic, and sauté till onion is translucent, about 3 to 4 minutes.

In a large mixing bowl, combine pasta, onion and garlic, spaghetti sauce, basil, ¾ cup of cheese, and vegetables. Transfer to a 13 × 9-inch baking dish and sprinkle with the remaining cheese.

Bake for 20 to 25 minutes or till heated through.

PER SERVING:
361 Calories; 15g Fat; 15g Protein; 42g Carbohydrate; 4g Dietary Fiber; 34mg Cholesterol; 178mg Sodium. Exchanges: 2 Grain (Starch); 1 Lean Meat; 2 Vegetable; 2½ Fat.

SERVING SUGGESTION: Serve with a big green salad.

Another Salad (Side) Bar

Sometimes it's hard to come up with new ideas for green salads. I give you different lists to choose from when building your tossed salad in another sidebar (see page 253). Those goodies will add texture, flavor, and variety to your salads.

But there is another consideration you should keep in mind when building your salad. A good salad is a colorful salad. Color is the nutritional gauge of a healthy salad. You want your salad to be in living color!

Let's start with the basis of your salad: the lettuce. And lettuce is green, right? The darker the green, the better. You want bright green—green like spinach, mâche, baby salad greens—all of these lettuces and leaves tell you they're brimming with nutrition.

Then there is orange and yellow, the indicator of big beta carotene ahead. Peppers, carrots, and squash are all vital veggies for this colorful contender. Don't forget to go for red, too. Tomatoes contain the all-important phytochemical lypocene, which helps fight cancer. Beets and radishes are great, as well. Think of other colors, too, found in fruits like blueberries, raspberries, and grapes—they make great nutritional accents in a big strapping salad and add a signature flavor you won't get otherwise.

Just remember—the more colorful your salad, the more healthful and nutritious you've made it. Remember to slice, sliver, grate, and shred your veggies for greater interest and texture. It doesn't take much to make a good salad great!

TOFU SURPRISE

Serves 6

"I was the one that was surprised! I looked at the ingredients and thought I wouldn't like it—boy, was I wrong! It was tasty, easy to make, and even my fussy DS ate it!"   —Karen

6 cups cooked long-grain brown rice
¼ cup low-sodium soy sauce
¼ cup lemon juice
2 tablespoons olive oil
1½ pounds firm tofu, cut into 1-inch cubes
2 garlic cloves, pressed
1 large onion, finely chopped
8 ounces mushrooms, cleaned and sliced
½ cup chopped unsalted dry-roasted peanuts
4 tablespoons pimientos
10 ounces watercress, rinsed and stems removed (or use spinach)

Fluff and keep rice warm.

In a large bowl, combine soy sauce, lemon juice, and 1 tablespoon olive oil. Add tofu and toss to coat; marinate for 10 minutes.

In a large skillet, heat remaining 1 tablespoon olive oil over medium-high heat. Add garlic and onion, and sauté for 1 minute. Lower heat; add mushrooms and the marinade from tofu and cook, covered, for 5 minutes. Add peanuts, pimientos, and tofu and simmer, covered, for another 5 minutes. Stir in watercress and simmer, covered, for about 1 minute, till watercress wilts. Serve over rice.

PER SERVING:
447 Calories; 17g Fat; 20g Protein; 58g Carbohydrate; 7g Dietary Fiber; 0mg Cholesterol; 433mg Sodium. Exchanges: 3½ Grain (Starch); 3 Lean Meat; 1 Vegetable; 0 Fruit; 2½ Fat.

SERVING SUGGESTIONS: Serve with a spinach salad and steamed baby carrots.

LATE-AUTUMN MEDLEY

Serves 6

2 tablespoons olive oil

2 medium onions, chopped

3 garlic cloves, pressed

1 large acorn squash, peeled and cut into 1-inch cubes

1 large sweet potato, peeled and cut into 1-inch cubes

1 (14.5-ounce) can diced tomatoes

1 teaspoon dried marjoram

¾ teaspoon cumin

Salt and pepper to taste

1 (15-ounce) can black beans

1 cup frozen corn kernels, thawed

3 tablespoons lime juice

In a large skillet, heat oil over medium heat. Add onions and garlic and cook, stirring occasionally, for 5 minutes, till onion is soft.

Stir in squash, sweet potato, tomatoes, marjoram, cumin, and salt and pepper. Bring to a boil over medium heat. Lower heat and simmer, covered, for 40 minutes or until squash is tender. Stir in beans and corn, and cook for about 5 minutes, till heated through. Stir in the lime juice.

PER SERVING:
207 Calories; 6g Fat; 7g Protein; 35g Carbohydrate; 8g Dietary Fiber; 0mg Cholesterol; 324mg Sodium. Exchanges: 2 Grain (Starch); ½ Lean Meat; 1 Vegetable; 0 Fruit; 1 Fat.

SERVING SUGGESTIONS: Serve with quesadillas (see page 258) and a big green salad.

EGGPLANT BAKE

Serves 6

2 large eggplants, cut into ¾-inch-thick rounds
Salt
¼ cup olive oil
2 large onions, chopped
1 teaspoon cumin
1 tablespoon red pepper flakes
1 cup white wine (or use white grape juice, with a splash of vinegar)
1 (28-ounce) can diced tomatoes
2 garlic cloves, pressed
½ cup currants
3 tablespoons chopped cilantro

Preheat oven to 400 degrees F.

Place sliced eggplant on a tray, and sprinkle generously with salt. Set aside for 20 minutes.

In a large pan, heat 2 tablespoons of oil over medium heat. Add onions and cook for about 5 minutes, till softened. Add cumin and red pepper flakes, and stir for 1 minute. Add wine and bring to a boil; reduce heat and simmer for 10 minutes, or till the mixture is reduced to one-fourth its size. Add tomatoes. Bring to a boil; reduce heat and cook for 10 minutes. Add garlic and currants. Simmer for 5 minutes. Remove from heat.

Rinse eggplant rounds and thoroughly dry by squeezing them between paper towels. In a large skillet, heat 2 tablespoons remaining oil over medium heat. Fry eggplant rounds for 3 to 4 minutes, turning to cook on both sides. Drain on paper towels.

In a large baking dish, layer eggplant rounds and tomato mixture, sprinkling cilantro between layers. Finish with a layer of eggplant. Bake for 30 minutes.

PER SERVING:
222 Calories; 10g Fat; 4g Protein; 28g Carbohydrate; 7g Dietary Fiber; 0mg Cholesterol; 205mg Sodium. Exchanges: 0 Grain (Starch); 0 Lean Meat; 3½ Vegetable; ½ Fruit; 2 Fat.

SERVING SUGGESTIONS: Serve with a Greek Salad (see page 256) and whole-grain rolls.

LEEK AND POTATO
CRUSTLESS QUICHE

Serves 6

2 tablespoons olive oil

3 medium leeks, rinsed well and sliced ½-inch thick

2 large potatoes, cut into ½-inch cubes

Salt and pepper to taste

⅓ cup water

2 large eggs

1 large egg white

1 cup skim milk

½ cup small-curd cottage cheese

3 tablespoons grated Parmesan cheese

Preheat oven to 325 degrees F. Lightly grease a 10-inch quiche dish or pie plate.

In a skillet, heat oil over medium heat. Add leeks, potatoes, and salt and pepper and cook, stirring, for 1 minute. Add water and simmer, covered, for 12 minutes, stirring occasionally.

Meanwhile, in a large bowl, combine eggs, egg white, milk, cottage cheese, and 2 tablespoons Parmesan cheese. Add the leek mixture and stir to combine. Pour into greased dish and sprinkle with remaining Parmesan cheese. Bake for 30 minutes or until set.

PER SERVING:
169 Calories; 8g Fat; 9g Protein; 17g Carbohydrate; 1g Dietary Fiber; 75mg Cholesterol; 188mg Sodium. Exchanges: ½ Grain (Starch); 1 Lean Meat; 1 Vegetable; 0 Non-Fat Milk; 1 Fat.

SERVING SUGGESTIONS: Serve with broccoli slaw and whole-grain rolls and butter.

CHEESY RICE CASSEROLE

Serves 6

1 tablespoon olive oil
2 large onions, chopped
2 celery stalks, thinly sliced
2 garlic cloves, pressed
1 tablespoon grated ginger root
1 tablespoon cumin
Salt and pepper to taste
2 cups long-grain brown rice
¼ cup oil packed sun-dried tomatoes
1 (28-ounce) can diced tomatoes
3 cups low-sodium vegetable broth
8 ounces mushrooms, cleaned and sliced
8 ounces fresh spinach, rinsed and chopped
2 cups shredded Cheddar cheese

In a skillet, heat oil over medium heat. Add onions and celery and cook for about 5 minutes, till softened. Add garlic, ginger root, cumin, salt and pepper, and rice; cook, stirring, for 1 minute. Add sun-dried tomatoes, canned tomatoes, and vegetable broth; bring to a boil.

Place mushrooms in slow cooker. Pour rice mixture over mushrooms and stir to combine. Place two clean dish towels (folded in half so you have four layers) across the top of the slow cooker. (The collected moisture will affect the consistency of the rice, and the towels will absorb the moisture.) Cover and cook on low for 7 to 8 hours or on high for 3 to 4 hours, until rice is tender and has absorbed the liquid.

Remove the towels, stir in spinach, and sprinkle cheese over mixture. Cover and cook on high for 20 to 25 minutes, till spinach is wilted and cheese melts.

PER SERVING:
497 Calories; 17g Fat; 24g Protein; 64g Carbohydrate; 8g Dietary Fiber; 40mg Cholesterol; 794mg Sodium. Exchanges: 3 Grain (Starch); 2 Lean Meat; 2½ Vegetable; 2½ Fat.

SERVING SUGGESTIONS: Serve with a baby greens salad and whole-grain rolls.

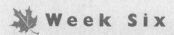 # Week Six

DAY ONE: Creamy Seashells

DAY TWO: Baked Potatoes Stuffed with Tofu

DAY THREE: Beany Tofu Barbecue

DAY FOUR: Portobello Reubens

DAY FIVE: Turnip Medley

DAY SIX: Albuquerque Sweet-and-Hot Potato Soup

SHOPPING LIST

CONDIMENTS

Olive oil

Vegetable oil

Dijon mustard

Barbecue sauce (16–18-ounce bottle) your favorite

Thousand Island dressing

**Salad dressing, your favorite (4 meals)

**Rice vinegar (2 meals)

**Mayonnaise (2 meals)

PRODUCE

2 (14–16-ounce) packages firm tofu

3 pounds yellow onions (keep on hand)

2 bunches green onions

2 garlic heads

Mushrooms (2 pounds)

6 large portobello mushroom caps

1 fresh jalapeño pepper

2 turnips

2 carrots; **additional 1 bag (1 meal)

3 large russet potatoes

5 sweet potatoes

1 bunch cilantro

4 limes (rind plus 2 tablespoons juice)

**Salad toppings (4 meals)

**Romaine lettuce (1 meal)

**Baby greens (1 meal)

**Spinach (2 meals)

**Baby carrots (1 meal)

**Coleslaw mix (1 meal)

**Grape tomatoes (1 meal)

CANNED GOODS

4 (14.5-ounce) cans low-sodium vegetable broth

1 (14.5-ounce) can diced tomatoes

1 (15-ounce) can chickpeas

1 (12-ounce) jar roasted red bell peppers

1 (14.5-ounce) can sauerkraut

SPICES AND DRIED HERBS

Basil

Thyme

Tarragon

Parsley

Oregano

Garlic powder

DAIRY/DAIRY CASE

Butter

Skim milk

Heavy cream (¾ cup)

Grated Parmesan cheese (5 tablespoons)

Shredded Cheddar cheese (1½ cups)

Swiss cheese slices (9 ounces)

**Blend of shredded Cheddar/Jack cheese (1 meal)

DRY GOODS
Large pasta shells (12 ounces)
Brown rice (3 cups)
**Raisins (1 meal)
**Walnuts (1 meal)

BREADS/BAKERY
6 whole wheat buns
**Whole-grain rolls (3 meals)
**Whole wheat tortillas (1 meal)

FROZEN FOODS
1 (20-ounce) package frozen corn kernels

CREAMY SEASHELLS

Serves 6

12 ounces large pasta shells
2 tablespoons olive oil
6 cups cleaned and sliced mushrooms
3 garlic cloves, pressed
3 teaspoons dried basil
Salt and pepper to taste
¾ cup heavy cream, not whipped
5 tablespoons grated Parmesan cheese
3 tablespoons sliced green onions

Cook pasta shells according to package directions until al dente. Drain and keep warm.

In a large skillet, heat oil over medium-high heat. Add mushrooms and garlic. Sprinkle with basil and salt and pepper. Cook 5 minutes, stirring frequently.

Add pasta to mushroom mixture and cook for 2 minutes. Add cream, cheese, and green onions and toss gently to mix.

PER SERVING:
394 Calories; 18g Fat; 11g Protein; 48g Carbohydrate; 3g Dietary Fiber; 44mg Cholesterol; 97mg Sodium. Exchanges: 3 Grain (Starch); 0 Lean Meat; 1 Vegetable; 0 Non-Fat Milk; 3 Fat.

SERVING SUGGESTIONS: Serve with a spinach salad and whole-grain rolls.

DO AHEAD TIP: If you want, go ahead and bake your potatoes for tomorrow night. That will make dinner for tomorrow a bit quicker!

BAKED POTATOES
STUFFED WITH TOFU

Serves 6

3 large potatoes, baked
1½ cups shredded Cheddar cheese
9 ounces tofu, sliced and drained well between paper towels
1 small onion, chopped
1½ tablespoons butter
1½ teaspoons Dijon mustard
½ teaspoon garlic powder
3 tablespoons skim milk
Salt and pepper
⅓ cup sliced green onions

Preheat oven to 400 degrees F. Scrub potatoes, poke them with a knife, and bake for 1 hour. Let cool enough to handle.

Cut potatoes in half lengthwise. Carefully scoop out pulp, leaving a ¼-inch shell.

In a large bowl, combine scooped-out potato with 1 cup cheese and all remaining ingredients except green onions. Mash with a fork or potato masher until well blended. Divide mixture evenly and fill the potato shells.

Place the potato halves in a greased baking dish and bake for 30 minutes. Garnish with green onions and remaining cheese.

PER SERVING:
191 Calories; 11g Fat; 10g Protein; 14g Carbohydrate; 2g Dietary Fiber; 28mg Cholesterol; 173mg Sodium. Exchanges: 1 Grain (Starch); 1 Lean Meat; 0 Vegetable; 0 Non-Fat Milk; 1½ Fat; 0 Other Carbohydrates.

SERVING SUGGESTIONS: Serve with a big romaine salad and baby carrots.

BEANY TOFU BARBECUE

4 garlic cloves, pressed

1 onion, chopped

2 teaspoons olive oil

1 (16–18-ounce) bottle barbecue sauce

1 (14.5-ounce) can diced tomatoes

1 (15-ounce) can chickpeas, drained

1 (14–16-ounce) package firm tofu, drained and cubed

6 whole wheat buns

In a large skillet, sauté garlic and onion in oil over medium heat until onion is translucent, about 3 to 4 minutes.

Stir in barbecue sauce and diced tomatoes. Add chickpeas and tofu. Stir and continue to cook till heated through. Serve on whole wheat buns.

PER SERVING:
377 Calories; 9g Fat; 17g Protein; 57g Carbohydrate; 8g Dietary Fiber; 0mg Cholesterol; 1117mg Sodium. Exchanges: 3 Grain (Starch); 1½ Lean Meat; 1 Vegetable; 1 Fat; ½ Other Carbohydrates.

SERVING SUGGESTIONS: Serve with coleslaw and grape tomatoes for the table.

PORTOBELLO REUBENS

Serves 6

6 *large portobello mushroom caps*
3 *tablespoons olive oil*
Salt and pepper to taste
1½ *cups sauerkraut*
9 *ounces Swiss cheese slices*
3 *tablespoons Thousand Island salad dressing*

Preheat the broiler.

Brush mushroom caps on both sides with olive oil and season with salt and pepper. Place the mushrooms in broiler pan, open side down, and broil for about 5 minutes. Turn and broil on the other side for 2 to 3 minutes.

Meanwhile, rinse and drain the sauerkraut, squeezing out as much water as possible.

Flip mushrooms back to open side up and fill with sauerkraut. Top with the Swiss cheese. Broil for 1 to 2 minutes, till cheese is melted.

Transfer mushroom caps to plates and spoon ½ tablespoon dressing on each.

PER SERVING:
291 Calories; 22g Fat; 15g Protein; 11g Carbohydrate; 3g Dietary Fiber; 41mg Cholesterol; 560mg Sodium. Exchanges: 1½ Lean Meat; 1½ Vegetable; 0 Fruit; 3 Fat.

SERVING SUGGESTIONS: Serve with Carrot Slaw (see page 254) and whole-grain rolls.

DO AHEAD TIP: Go ahead and get the rice cooked for tomorrow night's meal, then all you will have to do is heat it up.

TURNIP MEDLEY

Serves 6

1 tablespoon olive oil
3 garlic cloves, pressed
1 cup coarsely chopped onion
1½ cups peeled and diced turnip
1 cup sliced carrots
½ teaspoon dried thyme
¼ teaspoon dried tarragon
1 teaspoon dried parsley
Salt and pepper to taste
½ cup water
6 cups cooked brown rice

In a large saucepan, heat oil over medium heat. Add all ingredients except water and rice. Cook 5 minutes, stirring often.

Add water, reduce heat to low, cover, and cook 20 minutes or until vegetables are tender. Serve over rice.

PER SERVING:
291 Calories; 3g Fat; 6g Protein; 59g Carbohydrate; 3g Dietary Fiber; 0mg Cholesterol; 35mg Sodium. Exchanges: 3½ Grain (Starch); 0 Lean Meat; 1½ Vegetable; ½ Fat.

SERVING SUGGESTIONS: Serve with a baby greens salad and whole-grain rolls.

ALBUQUERQUE SWEET-AND-HOT POTATO SOUP

Serves 6

1 tablespoon vegetable oil

1 small fresh jalapeño pepper, chopped (discard ribs and seeds to
     bring the heat index down)

2 onions, finely chopped

4 garlic cloves, pressed

Salt and pepper to taste

1 teaspoon dried oregano

4 cups peeled and diced sweet potatoes

6 cups low-sodium vegetable broth

2 cups frozen corn kernels, thawed

1 teaspoon grated lime zest

2 tablespoons lime juice

6 tablespoons jarred roasted red bell peppers, cut into thin strips

3 tablespoons chopped cilantro

In a large skillet, heat oil over medium heat. Add jalapeño and onion and cook, stirring frequently, until softened, about 3 to 4 minutes. Add garlic, salt and pepper, and oregano and cook for about 1 minute, stirring frequently. Transfer mixture to slow cooker.

Add sweet potatoes and broth, stirring to combine. Cover and cook on low for 8 to 10 hours or on high for 4 to 6 hours, until sweet potatoes are tender.

Strain vegetables, reserving broth. In a blender or food processor, purée vegetables with 1 cup reserved broth. When smooth, return sweet potato mixture, along with reserved broth, to cooker. Add corn, lime zest, and juice. Cover and cook on high for 20 minutes.

Garnish with red bell pepper strips and cilantro.

PER SERVING:
240 Calories; 3g Fat; 15g Protein; 41g Carbohydrate; 8g Dietary Fiber; 0mg Cholesterol; 538mg Sodium. Exchanges: 2 Grain (Starch); 1½ Lean Meat; 1 Vegetable; 0 Fruit; ½ Fat.

SERVING SUGGESTIONS: Serve with a nice big spinach salad and BBQ Quesadillas (see page 258).

SERVING SUGGESTION RECIPES

I have this "thing" about serving suggestions. Or I should say, I have this "thing" about Serving Suggestions when it comes to my books (that's their official moniker, hence the use of capital letters). I believe in non-recipe recipes as much as possible when preparing side dishes. Listen, if you're going to go to all the trouble of making dinner—chopping, measuring, cooking, etc.—you sure as heck don't need to go through it all again in the form of a side dish; you'll be eating by midnight at that rate. Life is too short for complicated side dishes!

My philosophy is that if you can keep the side dishes simple and painless enough, making dinner will be much easier to accomplish on a regular basis. Simple salads, steamed veggies, and the like are always my preferred Serving Suggestions, for two reasons: first, they're easy, and "easy" is a necessary component in helping to get dinner on the table in no time flat; second, they ratchet up the nutrition of the whole meal, big time. For both of these reasons, it's essential to make most Serving Suggestion nonrecipe-type side dishes.

However, there is always an exception to every rule, and it is for that reason alone this section even exists. I have a few very simple recipes for a few very simple side dishes that are tried-and-true.

Let's start with salads, and once we've worked our way through those, we'll handle the more complicated (but not really) stuff. Ready? Let's go!

YOUR BASIC TOSSED GREEN SALAD

To me, there is nothing better on the side than a well-dressed green salad. Sometimes a tossed salad is the only raw thing we eat that day. We need more raw foods, especially vegetables. There are so many ways to accomplish this goal, especially in today's grocery stores. Stores have done everything for you except toss it together at your table! You can buy any kind of lettuce, triple washed, freshly bagged, and ready to go. Ditto on the veggies: grated carrots and shredded cabbages, chopped squash, and just about anything else you could hope for. They are all right there, waiting be to nabbed and taken home. Honestly, the price isn't too horrific considering how easy these good-choice convenience foods make it to be healthy. Money well spent, in my opinion. Just re-member to skip the iceberg lettuce—there is nearly no nutrition in ice-berg lettuce, and there are so many other great options out there. In my grocery store, there is baby spinach, mâche, mixed baby greens, hearts of romaine, Italian mixes with radicchio and butter lettuces, to name a few. Not only do they have them in bags or clear plastic tubs, but I can also get them organic.

To make your tossed green salad extra-nutritious, you will want to add some other veggies. This is a good place to use up that half a bell pepper that you didn't need for a recipe; it's a good way to clean out the crisper. This is also another way to use up those tail-end bags of coleslaw mix, shredded carrots, and the like. My salads are almost never alike because I'm constantly cleaning out my crisper!

Salad Fixin's

If you want to do a little something extra to kick up the flavor of your salads, include some extra "fixin's." I sometimes give you a big hint in the Serving Sug-gestion; then again, sometimes I don't because I want you to do your Serving Suggestion your way (like Burger King, only different).

I've listed different things to add to your salad. These are all items I use in my own tossed green salads. Just choose from one or two lists, or one item from each of the three lists—it's totally up to you.

- *Salad Fixin' #1:* Add cheese—I like blue cheese crumbles, crumbled feta, shredded Cheddar, grated Romano or Parmesan cheese.
- *Salad Fixin' #2:* Add nuts—I like walnut and pecan pieces, pine nuts, pumpkin seeds, and slivered almonds.
- *Salad Fixin' #3:* Add something fun. I like to add a cut-up apple or pear if I am using blue cheese crumbles and walnuts. During the winter, when tomatoes are dismal, oranges can add a nice burst of flavor (especially to a spinach salad). Or try a dash of raisins, dried cranberries, dried blueberries, or even crunchy tortilla chips. My editor adds dried TVP crumbles—how's that for crunch? There are all kinds of fun things to add!

BASIC COLESLAW

I love coleslaw because it's nutritious, full of fiber, and delicious. What I don't like is the work of shredding a cabbage. Have you ever noticed that you almost never use an entire head of cabbage? I used to end up dumping half the head after I made coleslaw because it would go bad in my fridge. But not anymore. Now they have these delightful little bags of already prepared coleslaw (just the shredded cabbage part) in the grocery store. Those bags are great for salad making and stir-fries, and of course, for making coleslaw. Now I can make my coleslaw in about 5 minutes and so can you. This recipe is from the first *Saving Dinner* cookbook, but it warrants being repeated in this book, as it is a significant side dish in all my books.

> *1 bag shredded cabbage*
> *Mayonnaise (I use low-fat)*
> *Rice vinegar*

Pour as much coleslaw as you need into a bowl. Add a little mayonnaise (go easy), stir, and if it looks dry, add some more; if it looks about right, leave it. You don't want it swimming in mayo. Now add a touch of rice vinegar. The ratio I use is about 1 teaspoon vinegar to 1 tablespoon mayo—that should help you in your measuring. The rice vinegar is slightly sweet, so it gives the coleslaw that hint of sweetness without being over the top.

That's it! Now serve or refrigerate for later.

VARIATION

Asian Coleslaw. Use mostly mayo and a generous splash of toasted sesame oil, another splash of rice vinegar, a handful of chopped cilantro, and some dry-roasted peanuts for a to-die-for Asian-style coleslaw. You will want to taste this one as you go, and adjust it per your own taste buds. I like a lot of sesame oil and less mayo, but you might like it with more mayo.

BROCCOLI SLAW

A similarly quick experience in slaw making, just like Basic Coleslaw. Feel free to use the Asian Slaw variation on your broccoli slaw as well.

> *1 bag shredded broccoli*
> *Mayonnaise (I use low-fat)*
> *Rice vinegar*

Pour as much broccoli slaw as you need into a bowl. Add a little mayonnaise (go easy), stir, and if it looks dry, add some more; if it looks about right, leave it. You don't want it swimming in mayo. Now add a touch of rice vinegar. The ratio I use is about 1 teaspoon vinegar to 1 tablespoon mayo—that should help you in your measuring.

That's it! Now serve or refrigerate for later.

CARROT SLAW

Another quick and easy recipe that is mostly a nonrecipe and way worth the effort. You'll love this salad—it's not the old cafeteria stand-by!

1 bag shredded carrots (or grate carrots yourself)
Raisins
Chopped walnuts
Mayonnaise (I use low-fat)

Pour as much shredded carrots as you need into a bowl. Add a little mayonnaise (go easy), stir, and keep adding till it gets moist but not drenched in mayo. Now add a handful or two of raisins and nuts, stir again, and taste the salad. It should have enough lumps and bumps to make you happy. That's it! Now serve or refrigerate for later, like the other slaws.

VARIATION

Add some canned drained crushed pineapple as well—a little bit goes a long way.

POTATO SALAD *SANS* RECIPE (FROM *SAVING DINNER*)

Potato salad can be made very similarly to coleslaw. After you have boiled the potatoes and drained them, toss them in a large bowl with a little vinegar (apple cider is what I use for this task) while they're still warm. This will make them permeable to the dressing (which is just plain mayo—low-fat is what I use) and give you a better-tasting potato salad. Next, add mayo and chopped whatever-you-want. I like celery and onion in mine (about a 1-to-1 ratio) and sometimes a hard-boiled egg, but not always. Salt and pepper to taste and there you go. Perfect with many of the summer menus and easy to make—this is potato salad, not an event.

BLUE CHEESE PASTA SALAD

Once again, another nonrecipe salad. The idea here is to clean out your crisper of any veggies that need to go, toss them with cooked pasta (fusilli works best), and add your favorite vinaigrette (you can make mine or buy your favorite bottled variety) and blue cheese crumbles. That's it! Seriously! A delicious salad in no time.

GREEK SALAD

As a side salad, start with some romaine lettuce, sliced cucumbers, and quartered tomatoes. Toss with your favorite vinaigrette, either bottled or homemade, and sprinkle some feta cheese right over the top (if your grocery store carries any flavored kinds, try the sun-dried tomato feta—it's great in this salad!).

CAESAR SALAD

Another side salad that uses shortcuts to keep it easy and simple. Toss together a big bowl of romaine lettuce, packaged croutons, Caesar salad-style dressing (no anchovies), and grated Parmesan cheese. Don't forget a liberal grinding of fresh pepper!

FAST AND EASY BUTTERMILK CORN MUFFINS (FROM *SAVING DINNER*)

My preference is corn muffins rather than cornbread—it's just easier. There's less mess (especially if you use cupcake liners), and the leftovers are easily frozen for another time.

1 cup cornmeal (I like white, but I think that's only available in the
*   South)*
1 cup whole wheat pastry flour (available at health food stores)
2 teaspoons baking powder
1 teaspoon baking soda
2 eggs, lightly beaten
¾ cup buttermilk
½ cup honey
4 tablespoons vegetable oil

Preheat oven to 375 degrees F. Line a muffin pan with cupcake liners.

In a large bowl, combine dry ingredients. Add the eggs, buttermilk, honey, and oil and mix until blended. Pour batter into muffin tins, two-thirds full.

Bake for 15 to 25 minutes, or until a light golden color. Let cool for a minute in the tin, then pull the muffins out to cool on a rack.

OVEN FRIES

Honestly, oven fries couldn't be easier, and they're a huge hit with the kids, too.

Large mealy potatoes (like russets, Yukon Golds, or Red Rose) cut
*   into steak fries or cut in half, if small*
Olive oil (not virgin)
Salt and pepper

Preheat oven to 400 degrees F.

Place cut-up potatoes in a large mixing bowl, pour a little olive oil over the top, and toss. I use my (clean) bare hands. Now add more oil if they seem a little dry—you don't want them drenched, but you want them to at least shine a bit. (It is preferable you don't have a big pool of olive oil hanging out at the bottom of your bowl.) Once your taters are glistening, salt and pepper them to taste, and toss again.

Lay your cut potatoes out on cookie sheets or jelly-roll pans. Bake about 20 minutes (depending on the size) or until they start to turn golden. Pull them from the oven and flip them over with a spatula, and put them back in the oven for an additional 10 to 20 minutes, depending on how done they are. That's it! Easy and good!

VARIATIONS

Garlicky Oven Fries. Sprinkle garlic powder on at the same time as you're doing the salt and pepper.

Sweet Potato Fries. Peel the sweet potatoes, then follow the recipe. For fun, use a little ground cinnamon instead of pepper.

BASIC QUESADILLAS

Quesadillas are like Mexican grilled-cheese sandwiches—same thing, just use tortillas (whole wheat or corn). To make them, simply spread a little butter on the tortilla, place it in a hot skillet over medium-high heat, and sprinkle shredded cheese over the tortilla (I use a combination of Cheddar and Jack cheeses). Top the cheese with another tortilla, also buttered, with the buttered side up. When the cheese is nice and melty, use your spatula to turn it over to cook on the other side. You want your quesadilla golden brown and the cheese satisfactorily melted.

VARIATIONS

Tex-Mex Quesadillas. Add a spoonful of your favorite salsa spread over the cheese before topping with the other tortilla.

BBQ Quesadillas. Add sliced onion and a dollop of your favorite barbecue sauce spread over the cheese before topping with the other tortilla.

BRAISED KALE, SWISS CHARD, COLLARDS, AND OTHER HEARTY GREENS

Braising is one of my favorite ways of doing greens. It's simple and delicious, and heartily recommended for greens as it cuts down cooking time and keeps the nutrients from leaching out, as traditional boiling would have you doing.

First, wash your greens then derib and de-stem them. Use a knife or your hands to get rid of the nasty, stringy rib. Now steam the greens in a covered skillet till crisp-tender. (You will need about 2 inches of water in your skillet.) When the greens are done, remove from the skillet, drain the water, and add a little olive oil to the pan. Heat the pan over medium-high heat for a few minutes, add the steamed greens and salt and pepper to taste (a little garlic if you like, too, at this point), and stir-fry the greens for about 3 minutes. They will be delicious and tender, but not overcooked. Enjoy!

HUMMUS

Put your blender or your food processor out on your countertop. You're halfway there in making hummus—it's that easy!

> 1 (15-ounce) can chickpeas, rinsed and drained
> ¼ cup tahini (found in the ethnic food section of your grocery store)
> ½ lemon, juiced (no seeds!)
> 1–2 garlic cloves, pressed
> ½ tablespoon olive oil
> Salt and pepper to taste

Throw everything into your blender or food processor and mix till smooth. That's it!

INDEX

Leanne Ely is considered *the* expert on family cooking and healthy eating. She is a syndicated newspaper columnist (The Dinner Diva), a certified nutritionist, and the host of SavingDinner.com. Leanne has a weekly "Food for Thought" column on the ever-popular FlyLady.net website, as well as her own e-zine, *Healthy Foods*. She is the author of *Saving Dinner, Saving Dinner the Low-Carb Way, Saving Dinner for the Holidays*, and *Saving Dinner Basics*. She lives in North Carolina with her two teenage children.